The People's History

Consett

A Commemoration of The Works

by

Tommy Moore

Copyright © Tommy Moore 2000

First published in 2000 by

The People's History Ltd
Suite 1
Byron House
Seaham Grange Business Park
Seaham
Co. Durham
SR7 0PY

ISBN 1 902527 43 7

Contents

Foreword

When Consett Steelworks closed on 12th September 1980 it was a devastating blow with a direct loss of over 4,500 jobs with a knock-on effect of approximately a further 5,000 job losses. It was horrifying.

Male unemployment hovered around 40% with almost every family in the Consett area being personally affected. Morale in the town was low, with little prospect of new industry replacing old. Eventually we were to lose our railway link, it was like having your main artery severed and being left to bleed to death. The ghost town scenario was considered by some to be a reality as people continued to leave the area, looking for work as had been happening because of pit closures. Indeed, the population continued to drop from over 110,000 to less then 85,000.

A very vigorous programme of regeneration was introduced with the District Council and Durham County Council both pressing for urgent and effective measures to combat the effects of closure. A delegation presented a strong case to the government for new development; reclamation works; improvement of road communications and a retraining programme. The scale of the problem was enormous and an integrated strategy was put in place to get Derwentside back on its feet.

Derwentside District Council believes that the policies it has pursued are now bearing fruit and are a practical example of the benefits of partnership. The Council has performed a necessary role as provider of services where the private sector would not step in because the wealth base of the community was not great enough to support its activities in leisure, housing and provision of business units. It is impossible to provide a comprehensive list of all that has been achieved but the following provides a flavour of the progress made over the last twenty years:

Over 6,300 jobs have been created; unemployment has come down to less than 8%; over £150 million of investment has been attracted to Derwentside; the population is now over 88,000 and growing.

Derwentside now enjoys all the advantages of a rapidly developing economy in a rural setting. A new breed of modern industries has been attracted through a vigorous Industrial Development Programme. The cultural, entrepreneurial and business acumen which caused Consett to rise to its historic heights were further harnessed for the future benefits which we now enjoy and will continue to be exercised. The area has a great deal to offer in terms of lifestyle and opportunity in a region attracting major international investment.

Alexander Watson
Executive Leader
Derwentside District Council

The riggers, fitters and blacksmiths of the Fell Coke Works Blacksmiths' Shop, 1921. Included are: Jack D'Eath, Bob Rudd, Bill Ellison, Sid Heaviside, Bob Sheriff, Jack Hannon, Charlie Brown, Tommy Harrison, Alf Elliott, Jack Gallagher, Bob Michall, Tom Francis, Jim Heatherington, Bob Wyatt, Tommy Martin, Jack Wyatt, Jim Willis, George Bell, Billy Dent and Billy Stafford.

Acknowledgements

Whilst every effort has been made to contact and acknowledge due copyright within this book, I would like to thank those copyright holders of any material contained within this publication where this has not been possible.

A note of a special acknowledgement is offered to my wife Norma, without whom the work would not have been completed, British Steels, General Steels Record Office, Derwentside District Council and the Derwentdale Local History Society.

Acknowledgement is also offered to the Reverend John Eyles, former Industrial Chaplain at the Consett Works during the final years of employment. Also to Bill and Nancy Johnson for their contribution and to George Nairn and Keith Stafford for the use of photographs.

Special thanks to Derek Laidler of Rufus Abajas for the cover design.

Introduction

It was largely the manufacture of iron and later of iron, steel and coal, that Consett was said to owe its growth. The hidden success, of which few realise, was of its blended cultures of people from every corner of the United Kingdom and abroad.

In little over a century, Consett developed from a small village of a few cottages to a large prosperous and important community whose products and name had become known throughout the world.

That there had been many earlier attempts at iron smelting in the area cannot be denied, one example being that of the Shotley Bridge Sword Makers of the seventeenth and eighteenth century.

At one time 'The Works' employed some 6,000 people. Eventually it was to cover over 650 acres and comprised of Cokeworks, Blast Furnaces, Steel Melting Shop, Plate Rolling Mills, Slabbing, Blooming and Billet Mill, complete with ancillaries, including a Power Station, Foundry, Brickworks, Fabrication, Engineering and Welding Shops. In addition there were the Technical Research Department, Locomotive Depots, extensive railway network and rolling stock.

Until 1947, when they were brought under Government ownership and nationalised, the Consett Iron Company had owned 37 coal mines during its 80 year history and whose geographical area spread from Langley Park to High Spen.

It is therefore fitting to briefly examine how that early settlement and early industries grew together into the present but rather isolated town which owes its existence to the vast modern complex of heavy industry which is still indelibly marked in the minds and consciences of many people.

It was largely due to this being the 'Year of the Millennium' and it also marked the twentieth anniversary of the closure of the iron and steelworks complex in Consett that it was decided to make a record, not only of the culture, the business acumen and the community which grew up with that industry about them, but also as a record to posterity and the younger generations who now have little to remind them of the industry which brought their forebears to the area of Consett.

Much of the technical data and photographic imagery included in this book are contained in the House Magazine of the Consett Iron Company which were freely issued during the years from 1957 to 1968.

It is the indelible imprint of many memories which everyone has, that are brought to life for a commemoration of the twentieth anniversary of the Works' closure.

Many thanks are extended to everyone for their kindness and in particular to British Steels, General Steels, for their kind permissions for the use of the Consett Iron Company House Magazines.

In particular, the permission of the Reverend John Eyles, Industrial Chaplain at the Consett Works at the time of the closure for his 'Diary of a Closure' is greatly appreciated. Many who read his account of the last year of production and the closure will attest to a profound account of the times.

To write a detailed history of iron and steel making would be pointless in relation to the history of the Consett Iron Company (or B.S.C. Works, Consett) as it was known at the time of closure, without even a minor recollection of memories, reminisces and stories of the camaraderie and community spirit which still abound today in those who worked there. This was a very real and palpable experience to those who were there.

By 1967, control of the steel industry by central Government brought Consett into the 'Northern & Tubes Group, British Steels Corporation'. Many of the research and development and quality control techniques which had historically been used to advantage by Consett Iron Company were released to other parts of the steel industry. This was to have an effect on the continuing success of the Consett Works.

Another effect on the Consett Works was its distance from a deep water harbour and associated costs in transport. Remembering that Consett's own ore supplies had largely run out by 1851-2, causing an importation of ore, firstly from Cleveland, and later from many distant parts.

Under rationalisation plans it was decided to close the Hownsgill Plate Mill in October 1979. It was thought at the time that the other parts of the Consett Works would continue production. This was denied as shortly after the closure of Hownsgill, it was announced that the entire Works was to close by September 1980.

The Consett Iron Works, as they have always been called – although one reference book gives 'Conside Iron Works' – have indeed known many changes and ups and downs since the days of the Derwent Iron Company in 1840. Perhaps the greatest down was the closure of the main economic base of North West Durham.

Over the years, many have left the area and still others have passed on, each with that unique memory and reminisce of their work. This book is not intended to be so much a record of the Works, but of those people who were employed, many times under very difficult conditions and in all weathers to produce steels which are still renowned throughout the world. To the reader, who does not have memory of the Works, it is trusted that some small part of this book will give you an insight into the industry. To those who do have memory of their times at work, it is hoped that some thought is brought to mind of the camaraderie and sense of community that existed in the among the workforce of Consett Iron Works.

As a final word, may I offer my sincerest apologies and regrets at not having mentioned some of the departments within the Works who themselves were indeed as much a major part of the Works as any other. Having worked there for some twenty-three years and known a great number of friends, it is with a certain sadness that to have given every department their full entitlement, this book could have run to many volumes.

It is with those sincere memories and good wishes that I acknowledge the work done by everyone. I therefore dedicate the book to everyone who ever worked and played there (when they had time!). To those who, in those immortal words, gave their blood, sweat, toil and tears, and indeed their lives in some instances, to earn a living.

Tommy Moore
Consett, September 2000

A BRIEF HISTORY OF CONSETT IRON COMPANY

The General Offices of the Consett Iron Company.

It was in 1839 that the idea of the Consett Ironworks was born. At that time, Consett consisted of the Delves House, Barrhouse and Carr House and a few thatched cottages somewhere near the area where Sherburn Terrace now stands. In fact, Consett was an isolated sparsely populated and mainly agricultural and rural landscape.

At that time, a William Richardson of Sunderland was staying at Shotley Spa, some short distance away. Mr Richardson became acquainted with a local mineral expert John Nicholson. These two gentlemen examined jointly some outcrops of ironstone in the district and took samples which were analysed and found to be satisfactory. Later, Robert Wilson of Newcastle was drawn into the picture, and together with Mr Richardson and Mr Nicholson arrangements were made for a number of shafts to be sunk. The first shaft being near what is now known as 'Number One' at the junction of Medomsley Road and Villa Real Road, Consett.

The results of this preliminary work must have been successful because in 1840 four partners, three of them Quakers, raised £10,000 to manufacture pig iron from the ironstone at Consett.

Almost immediately after the formation of the 'Derwent Iron Company' in 1841 the decision was taken to expand the Company to include puddling, rolling and finishing mills as well as the original two blast furnaces. This was done for the very good reason that it was found that bar iron was more easily marketable, and at a better profit, in addition to the ordinary pig iron.

The Derwent Iron Company really formed the foundations upon which the Consett Iron Company was built. This early company took out leases of ironstone and coal royalties at Consett, Delves and Hownsgill; and time and again in the history of the Works showed the prudent management of that original company been proven. In fact, time and again, the reason for the Works ever to be located at Consett and for their continuance there, was proved to be due to the existence of the local coal and not the ironstone.

The Derwent Iron Company began to expand rapidly. About this time the Redesdale Ironworks, which had been established since 1838, made an offer to join the Company. Although, for some reason, there was at first some opposition, but the amalgamation was finally carried through. Also at this period, the Company purchased the old Bishopwearmouth Works from the original founders, Messrs White, Panton and Co.

After this quick expansion and obvious success the ironworks then experienced almost two decades of trouble. Abundant coal which could be worked at between 2/- and 2/6d per ton (about 10p and 12^1/2p per ton decimal) was available in the district.

But it was found almost immediately that, although ironstone was plentiful in the Consett area, the reserves, after the initial pockets had been worked out, were difficult and

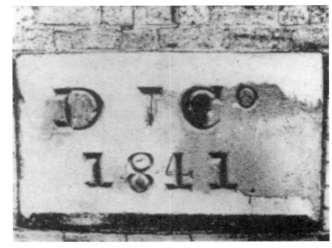

The original corner stone of the Derwent Iron Company.

Hownsgill Viaduct, built in 1857 to carry rail traffic from the Works.

uneconomic to work, and that local ironstone was costing about 10/- per ton delivered at the Works.

Alternative sources of supply were sought and these were found to be available from Cleveland and Cumbria. It was, in fact, cheaper to haul ironstone to Consett from these districts in spite of the carriage. It could be obtained from, for example, Cleveland at about 7/- per ton delivered to Consett. It is interesting to note the routes by which this ironstone reached Consett; the Cleveland ironstone travelled via Bishop Auckland and then over a series of rope inclines, whereas the Cumberland ironstone was brought via Carlisle and Redheugh. Some of this ironstone traffic had, of course, to pass over the ravine at Hownsgill and, until the Hownsgill Viaduct was opened on 1st July 1858, great problems were experienced in the transport of rail traffic across the gorge.

In November 1857 disaster struck the Derwent Iron Company. The Northumberland and District bank stopped payment and it became known that the Company was involved with the bank in the sum of nearly £1,000,000 – the actual figure being £986,831 0s 6d. Although the Works were stopped for a time, every effort was made by a number of shareholders in the bank and in the railway companies to save what they could from the wreck and try to get started again.

An engraving of the Consett & Derwent Iron Works, 1858.

An etching of the earliest pictorial record of Blast Furnaces at Consett. The horse-drawn railway dates it about 1860 and before CIC had steam locos. By 1872 steam power was introduced.

It was obviously a matter of first importance to the railway companies that the Works should be kept going, using as they did some 500,000 tons of coal and over 5,000,000 tons of ironstone and limestone; in addition the Works were turning out about 150,000 tons of finished goods each year. After protracted and difficult negotiations a further company, the Derwent and Consett Iron Company Ltd was formed in July 1858, with a capital of £150,000. A scheme was carried through whereby the assets of the Derwent Iron Company were transferred to the new company for, it is said, approximately £825,000 – at first sight a remarkable piece of accountancy. The following month, August 1858, the transfer to the new company began; progress must have been very slow because nearly two years later the transfer had not been completed, although the capital of the new company had been increased from £150,000 to £166,000. It is believed that the Works were stopped again for some time. By this time, say the middle of 1860, the Works at Consett included 18 blast furnaces, of which seven were at Consett, seven at Crookhall and four at Bradley; rolling mills, collieries, coke ovens and foundries and engine shops.

The changes in the ownership of the Works were not finished; the Derwent and Consett Iron Company Ltd were unable to complete the purchase, and the whole of the undertaking was put up for sale and was bought by the new Consett Iron Company Ltd, which was formed in April 1864. The capital of the new company was then £400,000 divided into 40,000 shares of £10 each. The original directors were Mr H. Fenwick of Chester-le-Street; Mr J. Henderson MP of Leazes House, Durham; Mr J.E. Coleman of Tokenhouse Yard, London; Mr J.W. Pease of Darlington; Mr J. Fogg Elliot of Durham; Mr T. Spence of the Grove, Ryton; Mr N.J. Wilson of Sunderland; Mr J. Priestman of Shotley Bridge and Mr David Dale of Darlington, who had been associated with the Works since 1857. Mr Priestman was appointed Managing Director, Sir David Dale

'Crook Hall' – From where the modern township derived its name.

was later appointed Chairman in 1884, and died in 1906 after an association with the Works of nearly 50 years.

The circumstances of the transfer to the Company are interesting. The liquidators of the Derwent and Consett Iron Company Ltd insisted that the creditors of the bank should have the option of taking up half of the shares in the new company. The prospectus indicated that the coal royalties were such as enabled the cost of coal not to exceed 2s 9d per ton, and further that the average annual profit had been £35,000. The undertaking was conducted in the name of the new company with effect from 15th August 1864.

By the time the transfer to the Consett Iron Company was complete, the original Works had grown into a substantial undertaking. Besides the eighteen blast furnaces at Consett, Crookhall, and Bradley, which have already been mentioned, complete of course, with blowing engines although at this time only six of these furnaces, all at Consett, were working; in addition there were 99 puddling furnaces at Consett and a further 31 at the old Bishopwearmouth Ironworks; there were plate, angle and bar mills, 500 acres of freehold land, 1,000 freehold cottages, coal royalties and the usual ancillaries. The annual output was about 800,000 tons of pig iron and between 40,000 and 50,000 tons of finished iron.

In 1866 the tin plateworks, situated to the north of the ironworks and at the time owned by the Shotley Bridge Ironworks Ltd

Sir David Dale, Managing Director CIC, 1864-1869, MD until 1873 and Company Chairman from 1884-1906 when he died.

No 2 Cogging Mill as it was in the nineteenth century, showing the continuous development of steel technology.

were acquired, together with a further 27 puddling furnaces and three plate mills for the sum of £55,000 payable in instalments. These old tin plate works were more accurately called the Shotley Bridge Mills but were always known as the tin mills, although tin plates were no longer produced but iron plates, the latter being more in demand. The name 'tin mill' still clings to the site of the old mills as are the names tin mill to a number of roads.

A colliery, Blackhill Drift, was situated near to the roundabout at the bottom of Blackhill Bank, formerly known as Pasture Drift Road, was included among the assets. About the same time, the old ironworks at Bishopwearmouth were disposed of and the Works were concentrated at Consett.

In the autumn of 1866 there was a strike of the puddlers at the Works, apparently caused by a decision of management to enforce a reduction in wages of 10% in the puddlers' wages. Once again, history does not record how the strike was settled, but settled it was, although the ironworkers had laid the mills idle for two or three months. There was, in fact, a real depression.

From then on, the Consett Iron Company made much progress. Older blast furnaces were decommissioned as new ones were built with a capacity of producing 919 tons a week. Also during this period, steady development proceeded with the colliery side of the undertaking. The sinking of Westwood Pit was planned in 1868 with coke ovens, and work commenced two years later, the pit coming into production in 1872. The following year a lease of the Langley Park coal royalty was obtained and steps were taken to open up the coal, with Langley Park Colliery commencing work in 1876. The latter part of this era saw also the beginning of the building by the Company of a vast number of cottages and houses to accommodate the workmen; this project proceeded for many years.

1872 was a year that had far reaching effects on the development of the Company. Up to that date supplies of haematite ore had been obtained from Cumberland and Lancashire, but in 1872 the Company amalgamated with the Dowlais Iron Company, Herr Krupp of Spain, in the formation of the Orconera Iron Company Ltd. This company acquired large mines of haematite ore at Bilbao in Spain, which were developed by the construction of railways, shipping staithes, etc, at a cost of over £500,000.

The Steel Rail which 'Came Back Home' from America.

For many years the Consett Iron Company was guaranteed large supplies of haematite ore of excellent quality until in 1948 arrangements were made for the whole of the shares in the Orconera Iron Ore Company Ltd to be acquired by Altos Hornos de Vizcaya SA of Bilbao, Spain.

In connection with the 1872 scheme, the capital of the Company was further increased to £552,000 by the issue of 9,200 shares of £10 each. Owing to a technical difficulty in connection with the company's memorandum, a separate company, Consett Spanish Ore Company Ltd, was formed for the purpose of contributing a proportion of the capital required by the Orconera Company. Vast supplies of haematite ore must have been forthcoming from Spain very quickly because in 1874 and for nearly two years afterwards civil unrest prevented supplies being continued and yet the Company managed to 'live on its hump', in the form of reserves.

There is no doubt that in the earlier days the Company was helped greatly by the incidence of the railway era, with the consequent high demand for iron rails, which were, of course, produced by the Company. One interesting point is that early in the Second World War, a piece of iron rail marked Consett 1872, was found to be included in a shipment of scrap to the Company from America.

For a few years up to about 1876, the output of malleable iron plates and rails frequently reached 2,000 tons per week, but about 1876 came the extinction of the iron rail trade and the substitution of steel rails. There was a prompt and depressing slump. The malleable iron trade in the North of England was crippled almost overnight, the total output being reduced from some 600,000 tons per annum to nearly half that figure and output at Consett falling by one third. But the Company kept going by meeting the enormous and unparalleled demand for plates for iron ships, and for the next three years directed their entire efforts to that end, the weekly output of these plates at times being as high as 1,900

An old woodcut showing a Bessemer Converter for making steel. It was in 1857 that the process was patented. A process which made malleable iron.

tons. In order to obtain what was for those days a very large output there were in operation 170 puddling furnaces, ten steam hammers and seven plate rolling mills.

But times were hard up to 1880 and it is on record that in 1879 officials of the Company of all grades 'cheerfully acquiesced in a substantial reduction of their salaries' and the directors proposed to forego a portion of their allowance for that and the previous year. The financial position of the Company, however, was not only sound, but easy, and the following year the capital of the Company was further increased by the creation of an additional 18,400 shares of £10 each.

By 1882, however, it became clear that iron plates for shipbuilding were also outdated and would be substituted by steel plates made by the Siemens-Martin process. The Company accordingly decided to keep abreast of the times and to include the manufacture of steel in its operations. The impression must not be gathered that this development had taken the Company in any way by surprise. During the depression of 1876 the Company had been directing its attention to steel, and had continued to do this, so much so that in 1880 arrangements were made for the sum of £10,000 to be spent on experimental work in that matter. Visits to the then most up-to-date and economical steel plateworks by Mr W. Jenkins, the General Manager, resulted in him perfecting plans for erecting a small Siemens-Martin steel plant, and arrangements were made for this to proceed on a moderate but no longer experimental scale.

A start was made by the erection of two small 13-ton Siemens furnaces together with an 8-ton hammer and Siemens furnace for heating the ingots. This plant was put into operation in 1883 and the manufacture of steel plates from hammered ingots commenced. Shortly afterwards four larger furnaces, each of 19 tons capacity, and later another two of the same size were added.

These eight furnaces together with the Siemens gas furnace used for heating

No 8 Blast Furnace about 1912.

A view toward Blackhill with the Angle Mills on the left in 1890. This area is now the new road by-pass between Consett and Blackhill.

ingots for the hammer, constituted what became known as the West Melting Shop – this latter furnace being converted some time later into a 20-ton melting furnace. The furnaces must have proved successful because in 1887 a further nine melting furnaces, each of 25 tons capacity, were completed. In spite of work being held up for some time on account of severe weather, they formed the East Melting Shop. The top capacity of the West and East Melting Shops together being thus raised to about 3,500 tons per week. The chequers for all these furnaces were made by the Company from local ganister. At the same time a new steam-driven cogging mill, known as No 4, and capable of cogging 2,000 steel ingots per week, was erected to deal with the ingots from the East Melting Shop and Nos 3 and 4 Plate Mills were remodelled and strengthened.

In 1886 the capital of the Company was again increased by a further 26,400 shares of £10 each. It was now decided to meet the requirements of shipbuilders by supplying angles and other sectional steel, in addition to plates, and in 1888 work was started on the erecting of the Angle Mills to the north of the General Offices. The civil engineering work on this new site presented an unpromising picture, a situation as will be seen later by no means unusual at Consett. The site chosen, in fact the only convenient site available, was rugged and uneven, covered with heaps of slag and other refuse. And, as if these difficulties in themselves were not enough, with an inequality of upwards of 30 feet in some places. The task, however, began and slag was in some instances quarried to a depth of 35 feet. Massive retaining walls were built and hundreds of tons of non-combustible material tipped in order to bring the floors up to a proper level. These mills were finally put to work in 1893.

For a number of years, from 1888 onwards, trade was fairly good and the Company forged ahead. The Langley Park workings were extended and in 1890 Garesfield Colliery, together with railways and shipping quays, was purchased for £140,000; at the same time 100,000 preference shares of £5 each were issued.

On 11th August 1891, Consett Park was opened to the public and in the same year work began on the extension of the Derwenthaugh to Garesfield railway as far as the 'Chopwell New Winning'. One of the periodic recessions in trade then hit the Company and while profits continued to be made, these fluctuated. Matters were not helped by a decision of the Durham Coal

The East End of Angle Mills, built in 1888 and completed in 1893. The site was reconstructed after the First World War.

Trade to limit outputs, but the Company continued the work of development.

By 1893, the Company was a very large undertaking and was rapidly expanding. At that time ten collieries were being operated: Westwood, Medomsley, Derwent, Hunter, Eden, Blackhill, Delves, two at Langley Park and one at Garesfield, from which the annual output was in the region of 1,000,000 tons. Some of this was exported, particularly from Garesfield. A great deal was carbonised in 1,050 Beehive Coke Ovens which produced some 500,000 tons of coke annually. It has already been stated that there were seven Blast Furnaces, the East and West Melting Shops, Cogging Mills, Plate Mills, and, of course, what were then the new Angle Mills. There were, in addition, what were known as the North Melting Shops, actually in the Angle Mill Building, consisting of seven furnaces, each with a capacity of 25 tons.

The usual ancillaries were to be found. These were: the Foundry at

Garesfield Colliery, originally opened 1800. The colliery was purchased in 1890 by the CIC from the Marquis of Bute and a Miss Simpson. The purchase included railways and shipping quays.

Blackhill and Consett Park, opened 11th June 1891 by Mrs David Dale. The park covers 30 acres. It took 18 months to create and the total cost was £5,200.

Crookhall, which could at the time produce weekly 150 tons of castings; Delves Brickworks, with a capacity of some 120,000 bricks per week; Engineering Shops, Laboratory and Test House, Locomotive and Wagon Repair Shops, and the usual railways, rolling stock and ancillary plant.

Of the rolling stock, undoubtedly the 'E' Class Cranes were the most interesting, since these were specially built to the design of Mr J.P. Rowe, the Company's chief designer. That the design of these cranes was sound is proved by the fact that eleven of this class were still in use in the 1960s, most of them being well over sixty years old.

The General Offices, which had been built in 1884 were already being enlarged. Some 2,700 cottages were owned at Consett, Blackhill, Leadgate and the outlying districts. 6,000 hands were employed, the wages paid amounting to £8,000 per week or £416,000 per year. There were also schools and educational reading rooms at Consett, Blackhill, Leadgate, Allendale and Langley Park.

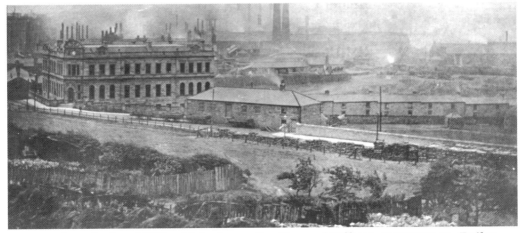

A scene from before 1890 which shows the General Offices, B Furnaces, Boiler Shops, Fitting Shops, No 4 Plate Mill and East and West Melting Shops. (Staffordshire Row can be seen below the offices.)

The Consett Infirmary, which was built between 1877 and 1879, was proving its worth to those who were unfortunate to be injured in the Works or the pits. In fact this building was used, so the story goes, before it was finished and equipped. The roof of one of the Mills collapsed, while the Infirmary was in course of construction, due to

The General Offices, circa 1890. Note the sloping ground on the right.

the heavy weight of snow. The men who were injured were taken to the unfinished Infirmary where, it is said, they had to be accommodated temporarily on straw palisades due to the fact that the building was not really ready to receive the equipment. Some accounts say that it was the Angle Mill roof that collapsed but this cannot be so, as work on that Mill was not started until some ten years later.

The Company now enjoyed a few years in which to proceed successfully with its normal business and to prepare by development against any difficulty years ahead. Satisfactory profits were made.

Chopwell Colliery and Coke Ovens were opened up and put to work,

The old Angle Mills.

The Works about 1895. A view looking from Berry Edge. The Old Pig Beds are on the left, Storehouse is centre right and the General Offices extreme right.

although this colliery was laid-up for some time in 1898 owing to a wages dispute. The extension of the railway to what became known as the Chopwell and Garesfield Railway was finished, the portion lying between Derwenthaugh and Garesfield being enlarged and the Derwenthaugh Quay was remodelled into the old Derwenthaugh Staithes.

In 1898 the Company acquired a piece of land on the right bank of the Tyne, below Scotswood Bridge, with the object of providing wharf accommodation for the discharge of imported ores. This piece of land again came under review forty years later for the same purpose, but, as will be told, arrangements were then finally made with the Tyne Improvement Commissioners for the ore to be handled at Tyne Dock.

The turn of the century was uneventful, although the question of a complete Works' reconstruction scheme was again under consideration and the General Works Manager, Mr Ainsworth, accompanied by the Chief Engineer, Mr Scott, visited iron and steelworks in America before settling finally on any plan.

The early banking history of the Works was unfortunate and now for the second time in their history they were involved in the collapse of a bank. This time it was J. and J. W. Pease's Bank, which stopped payment on 23rd August 1902. This crash did not, however, have any far reaching or disastrous effect on the Works, as was the case with the old Derwent Iron Company and the Northumberland and Durham District Bank in 1857, although the Company were forced, as a result, to write off £50,000.

Steady Progress

Some steady, but not rapid progress, was made in reconstruction work in particular on the Blast Furnace Plant, during the next few years. These years were mainly uneventful except for the building of the offices in Pilgrim Street, Newcastle, which were opened in 1905.

No 8 Blast Furnace.

The year 1906, however, was a remarkable one for three occurrences: first, the death of Sir David Dale after nearly fifty years' association with the Works; secondly, the setting to work of the Low Pond Pumps, which, as *The Engineer* for January of that year stated, had a total capacity of nearly 86,000,000 gallons every 24 hours, taking 30 gallons as representing an average consumption per head, this capacity would be sufficient for a town of over 286,000 inhabitants; thirdly, work was started on No 8 Blast Furnace. The furnace was completed in 1908 but owing to the state of trade was not blown until two years later.

The three years ending with 1912 saw the introduction of the eight-hour day into the collieries; a lock-out in the shipyards, a railway strike and a strike of miners on a national basis. But the Company managed to get a further fifty ovens at

Walter Pledger retires in 1957 after 50 years service.

Blast Furnace Top Men, 1915. Included are: John McKeown, Dennis Morris and Chris Winter (front row, extreme right).

Templetown Cokeworks into operation together with a Benzole Still. Work was commenced and finished in 1914 on a further extension to Derwenthaugh Staithes.

In 1913 the capital structure of the Company was again altered so that there were 1,000,000 ordinary shares of £1 each and 500,000 preference shares of a like amount.

The First World War

The following year the Great War came, with its attendant difficulties with which all are now so familiar. The period 1914-1915 was the Company's worst for twenty years and difficulties increased. Prices of raw materials, timber and stores soared, workmen enlisted in the forces so much so that in 1916 one of the largest Plate Mills was idle for some time – the collieries came under the Coal Controller, the output of coal decreased, maximum prices were fixed and the Works were brought under the control of the Ministry of Munitions.

Apart from these general national difficulties the Company had its individual troubles. A main flue at Templetown Cokeworks collapsed and one battery of ovens had to be put out, although opportunity was taken during the repairs to put in a new sloping cooling bench, and an accident to the engine of

SS Consett.

the largest Angle Mill stopped work for ten weeks. During this period Langley Park Coke Ovens were put to work (in 1915) to amplify the existing Templetown Ovens.

Aftermath

The Company and the Works survived although the next few years brought their own additional difficulties. A general reconstruction of the Works received active consideration and a visit was made to America to study the position there; but the bogey of nationalisation of the mines and the general uncertainty of the industrial position held up the scheme.

The introduction of the eight-hour day into the Steelworks and Rolling Plant interfered with production and at one time the Works were at a standstill for lack of coal. On the brighter side of the picture, work on the new Victory Pit was commenced and the Company acquired four steamers – SS *Consett*, SS *Knitsley*, SS *Garesfield* and SS *Blackhill* – in order to ensure a regular supply of ore to the Blast Furnaces. For a time the Company was riding the post-war trade boom and a further 2,000,000 fully paid ordinary shares of £1 were issued, but the boom collapsed and the Company found itself unable to compete without some modernisation of the Works.

In the early 1920s came one more example of the bold and comprehensive policy that was a characteristic of the Company since its inception. At a time,

SS *Knitsley*.

SS *Garesfield*.

SS Blackhill.

as has been seen, of general unrest and exceptional industrial depression – at a time when there seemed little to justify confidence in the future – it was decided to lay down new Plate Mills and at the same time to reconstruct and modernise the whole of the Plant. The Works were shut down except for part of the Blast Furnace plant and reconstruction began. The Blast Furnace plant was brought up to date, the Melting Shop was erected, new Steel Furnaces were built, together with the Plate Mills. The Angle Mills were modernised and extended; Templetown Brickworks were erected specially in order to supply bricks and shapes for a new Coke Oven plant at the Fell (the first all-silica coke oven battery in Europe), which was put to work in 1924, since when it operated continuously and efficiently until closure in 1980. Templetown Tar Distillation plant was also put down. Nor was the colliery side of the

Blast Furnaces, 1924. The furnaces, stoves, chimneys, crane gantry, pig beds ore and coke gears have all gone.

The Low Yard with the East and West Melting Shops in the background.

undertaking ignored. Victory Pit was got to work and a new winning opened at Humber Hill. And as if all this was not enough, continuous progress was made with the building of houses for the workmen.

Trading Conditions

In spite of all this enterprise and vast expenditure of money the trading conditions under which the Company operated for the next ten years made rather depressing reading, with almost a continuous tale either of falling demand or prices and rising costs. Part of the blame for these troubles must be laid at the door of the Government of the day, which encouraged the policy of rationalisation but refused to protect the home market. No sooner was the reconstruction basically complete than the Company was faced with a period of unprecedented trade depression, which resulted in considerable loss when the new plant was started up, coupled with tremendous labour difficulties culminating in the General Strike and a national coal stoppage.

Once again the Company did the unexpected and set to work in 1927 to lay down a new Coke Oven and By-Product plant at Derwenthaugh, having negotiated a very satisfactory contract for the sale of their products to the Newcastle and Gateshead Gas Company. This new plant was put to work in February 1929, the normal starting up difficulties being accentuated by the usual severe weather and a further ten ovens were added in December of that year. A coke nut depot was opened at Derwenthaugh for the delivery of coke nuts into Newcastle and district.

Depression

By 1931 the shipbuilding industry was experiencing its worst depression for many years. Coke was being put to stock owing to the fall in both price and demand while only two small blast furnaces were working in order to reduce the already considerable stocks of pig iron. In such circumstances, no larger integrated plant could show full results. The Chairman remarked to the shareholders of the Company at the Annual General Meeting on 17th June 1931, when reviewing the general situation, that: 'There surely can be no excuse for repeating the statement that the industry is not exerting itself to the utmost. On the contrary, it has for the past ten years been fighting a rearguard action for survival.'

By 1932 tariffs had been imposed on iron and steel and prospects of an improvement in trade were not regarded as entirely improbable. But the continued depression had imposed a severe strain on the Company's liquid resources and modifications were made to the debenture stock conditions. After a struggling but courageous era of development in 1936 a re-organisation scheme was carried through.

End Of A Campaign

On 5th July, No l Blast Furnace was blown out for relining after a campaign of nearly seven years, and with a total production of 1,413,286 tons of iron to her credit. The length of campaign and the tonnage produced compares more than favourably with the national average of the times.

In the following year work was started on the erection of a Gas Cleaning plant and a large gas holder. These units, which were put to work in April 1939, formed the first step in a contemplated modernisation of the whole Blast Furnace plant. But, in common with other iron and steelworks, some short time was being worked throughout the various departments and on 1st January 1939, heavy reductions in the price of pig iron and steel plates came into force.

The outbreak of the war in September 1939, gave a great impetus to production and full-time working was resumed while at the same time the whole of the iron and steel industry was scheduled by the Government as a controlled industry, a step which affected both the disposal and price of the Company's products.

May 1940 saw the starting up of a new Strip and Bar Mill at Jarrow, owned by the New Jarrow Steel Company Ltd. This particular project was the culmination of efforts by the Government to introduce some new industry into the distressed area of Jarrow.

It must be said to the credit of the Company that at a time when the whole of the iron and steel industry was in a state of depression, the Company went forward. They undertook ultimate financial responsibility for the scheme along with the Bankers Industrial Development Company Limited and the Nuffield Trust for the special areas.

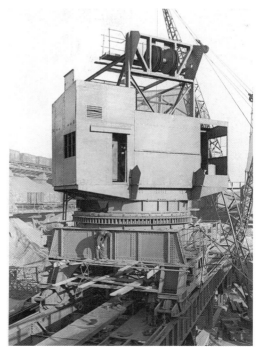

A jib crane at the Blast Furnace during rebuilding in 1941.

Work in progress during the Blast Furnace rebuild in 1941.

So heavy was the demand for the products of the mill, due to war requirements, that double-shift working was introduced almost immediately. Meanwhile, Consett was making its own contribution to the war effort and was indeed fortunate in that no serious bombing such as other industrial centres experienced took place, although of course there were the many hindrances to production imposed by black-out and other restrictions.

The directors of the Company realised that at the end of the war the Company would have to progress and the post-war plan for the industry in which the Company was to play its part in full, began to take shape. Indeed, at Consett, development was beginning to take place already. By the end of 1943, despite all the difficulties of wartime restrictions, a completely modern mechanically charged Blast Furnace (No 2) with a capacity of more than three times any of the old small furnaces had been installed. This was put into production together with new ore handling plant, sinter plant and a pig casting machine.

During the closing stages of the war the Consett plan had begun to take shape and post-war trends were being examined in order to make the very difficult decision as to the type of finished product upon which the Company should concentrate.

With the change from war to peace came a change of political thought throughout the country, and on 1st January 1947 the first of the Labour Party's nationalisation measures – The Coal Industry Nationalisation Act, 1946, which set up the National Coal Board to take the mining industry into public ownership, came into force. Under that Act there was, vested in the National Coal Board, a sizeable part of the Company's undertaking, including seven collieries (including: Victory Pit, Eden, Medomsley, Derwent) the Derwenthaugh and Langley Park Cokeworks, Crookhall Washery, the electricity generating and distribution system, with its four power stations at Derwenthaugh, Chopwell, Langley Park and Templetown, 3,500 houses, nearly 12,500 acres of land as well as over 50 miles of railways with rolling stock.

This amputation, as it were, of a limb of the Company could have proved a devastating blow but the Company survived and indeed actively continued day to day management of the assets transferred to the National Coal Board for nine months.

February and March of 1947 will be imprinted in the minds of many readers due to the heavy and persistent snowstorms which restricted supplies of fuel to the Works. This brought production almost to a standstill and dislocated the whole undertaking for some time.

In September 1947, a new large Blast Furnace (No 3), similar to No 2 was blown in, and three years later the last landmark of the old Blast Furnace Plant disappeared when the old No 8 Furnace and the large brick chimney which had been in existence for some 80 years was replaced by the third of the large new furnaces.

The final plan was now taking shape and Consett was beginning to get a 'new look'. Development was in progress everywhere and striking changes in the vista of the Works was obvious. The Central Power Station, a most impressive modern building housing five boilers, three turbo-alternators each producing 15,000 Kw, five turbo blowers, four of which were capable of dealing with 55,000 cubic feet of air per minute, were set to work in various stages between 1947 and 1950; 54 Becker Ovens at Fell Cokeworks were completed in May 1948 and further batteries of 17 and 20 Wilputte Ovens replacing old ones which had operated continuously since 1924, began producing coke in August 1953 and December 1955 respectively. During the middle of 1948 the Company exercised its option to acquire the balance of the share capital of the New Jarrow Steel Company Limited and the latter became wholly absorbed into the Consett administration.

Meanwhile, the conversion of the open hearth steel furnaces in the Melting Shop from 80 tons to 160 tons proceeded. The enlargement entailing the conversion to coke oven gas and tar oils as fuels so permitting the final scrapping of all the gas producers in the Works and making necessary a new coke oven gas holder with a capacity of one million cubic feet.

The next phase was to increase the finishing capacity of the Works with a type and throughput which had to be in conformity with the overall plan for the industry. It was considered that Consett's part in the national and regional scheme of production and the economy was to provide additional billet and slab rolling facilities.

The New Mill – a combined Slabbing and Blooming Mill and Continuous Billet Mill – was installed and put to work in 1953.

To meet the increased rolling capacity of the new mill it was necessary to increase ingot capacity and in the face of the world shortage of scrap it was decided to make steel by the Duplexing process and two Bessemer Converters were installed. To operate the three modern blast furnaces adequately and to serve the Duplex Plant, work was put into hand for a new ore handling plant, complete with ore terminal and discharge bunkers, two stocking out bridges and a reclaiming ore bridge. This was reputed to be the largest yet constructed anywhere outside America.

After protracted negotiations with British Railways and the Tyne Improvement Commissioners it was arranged that ore would be discharged by the most modern plant at Tyne Dock and loaded into trains of special 56-ton wagons provided by British Railways. Furthermore, the Sinter Plant, installed during the war was replaced by a continuous strand Dwight-Lloyd plant. A second strand was erected to bring sinter production to 15,000 tons per week.

In addition to the development planned for Consett it was decided to build a completely modern basic refractory brickworks on the riverside site beside the Jarrow Mill. These new brickworks commenced operations in May 1952. The total cost of development so far was in excess of £20,000,000, or nearly £3,000 per man employed, a measure of the large sums of money needed.

Politics were to have their impact upon the Company twice during this period with successive governments first nationalising then privatising the industry. On 15th February 1951, as a result of Labour's Iron and Steel Act, 1949, the whole of the share capital of Consett was vested in the Iron and Steel Corporation of Great Britain. On 12th December 1955, under the Iron and Steel Act, 1953, passed by the Conservatives, the Company reverted to private ownership.

In 1956 a new Foundry was constructed to the south of the old Plate Mill and work steadily progressed to construct a new four high Plate Mill at Hownsgill which was the biggest in Europe at the time and opened in 1961. This was followed by the construction of an Oxygen steelmaking complex, which was a marvel in innovation and business acumen little seen nowadays. The two types of Oxygen steelmaking were still very much under discussion at the time. Consett Iron Company decided to build both types in order to assess their individual economic benefits and/or failures.

The Linz-Donowitz (L.D.) process produced a shorter steelmaking cycle, but could not guarantee quality to the degree that the other process could.

On the other hand, the Kaldo process whilst producing good results was very heavy to run economically. It was decided to adopt the L.D. process and to produce high quality steels by the improvement of quality assurance techniques in the steel plant. This was achieved to such a degree that Consett could produce such qualities of steel that could not be produced anywhere around the world.

SECTION TWO

IMPORTING ORE, THE BLAST FURNACES & THE POWER STATION

T. Agar, T. Phillipson and E. Stokoe working on a slurry pump.

Imported Ore – From Tyne Dock To Consett

When the very considerable increase in iron and steel making was planned to follow the Second World War special consideration was given to modern handling from ship to stocking yard of the much increased quantity of imported ores that would be required – some 1¼ million tons per year.

Several alternatives were considered, centred on the Company's deep-water wharf at Derwenthaugh, seven miles up the Tyne.

Iron Ore being unloaded at Tyne Dock.

This wharf had serviced vessels up to 12,000 tons dead-weight carrying capacity and a scheme was adopted and approved by the several authorities concerned to install their modern ship discharge cranes. At the time, either a double aerial rope-way or conveyor belts to transport the ore to the Consett Works was planned, a distance of eleven miles.

Before work could actually start, however, the relatively newly appointed Dock and Inland Waterways Executive reviewed the port systems of the North East coast and any development schemes in hand or under consideration. This authority rejected the Consett Iron Company's scheme because of the limit to ship-size of 12,000 tons imposed by the local conditions, insisting that provision should be made for ore carriers not less than 20,000 tons. There was opposition too, as the Consett scheme would take business from the Tyne Improvement Commission and the British Transport Commission. A scheme

MV Ore Regent with a shipment of 31,000 tons of ore at Tyne Dock.

was approved, comprising the fundamental features of the Consett Company's scheme based on a new wharf twenty-two miles from the Works culminating in a tripartite agreement under which the Tyne Improvement Commission built a new deep-water quay dredged to thirty-five feet at low water, capable of taking ships of up to 25,000 tons at all states of the tide without grounding.

Equipped with modern discharging apparatus the plant was to be capable of handling the quantity of ore required by the Consett Iron Company. The new quay and plant was situated immediately westward of Tyne Dock entrance and, forming a continuation of an existing timber quay built in 1942, was brought into operation in November 1953.

Railways

A fleet of thirty 56-ton hopper wagons with power-operated doors, were put into service by British Railways. These worked in shuttle service in trains of nine wagons, leaving three spares, and did the work of about six hundred 21-ton bottom-door discharge wagons which had previously been used in the ore trade. The locomotives allocated to this circuit working were equipped with special control valves and piping to operate the wagon doors throughout the train from the footplate. During the winter months moisture freezing in the piping caused difficulty in opening the wagon doors.

When the trains left the Tyne Dock estate, they entered the British Railways system. The train loading was restricted to 500 tons. This maximum load was limited because of the gradients on the British Railways lines from Tyne Dock to Consett. These gradients varied from 1 in 48 to 1 in 114. From South Pelaw, the railways employed a banking engine to assist the train engine in negotiating a rise in gradient of 1 in 50 which persisted practically throughout to the Consett ore terminal.

The train schedules from Tyne Dock to Consett took about 1 hour 50 minutes. Usually fourteen trains per day were booked for ore traffic, conveying approximately 6,500 tons of ore. The trains were operated from 1.25 am to 11.25 pm.

One of the fourteen ore trains of nine wagons which ran daily from Tyne Dock to Consett via Boldon, Washington and Leadgate.

Ore Handling At Consett

The ore handling plant at Consett was very simple and included the terminal bunkers, conveyors, stocking and reclaiming bridges. The plant was designed to handle iron ore and limestone of maximum size lumps twelve inch cube. The railway approaches to the ore terminal were protected by a modern signalling system controlled from a signal box and worked by British Railways' personnel. The whole installation was capable of discharging and handling over 10,000 tons of ore per 24 hours.

The ore terminal comprised 22 bunkers, each capable of holding about 30 tons. The flow system was so arranged that each 56 ton railway wagon could discharge into two adjacent bunkers. The train of nine special wagons and the locomotive proceeded directly to the terminal. The safety catches of the wagons were released and when the train was positioned over the bunkers all doors were opened by the locomotive driver and the contents of the nine special wagons were discharged simultaneously into the bunkers below in a matter of seconds. Sixteen bunkers were used for the reception of ore. The remaining six were used for tipping limestone, dolomite, etc during the hours when ore trains were not been operated.

The locomotive reversed off the terminal through a triangle and then proceeded on its journey to Tyne Dock without detaching the locomotive. Tests showed that all these operations could be completed and the train be started on its way to Tyne Dock in under fifteen minutes.

Rubber belts took the ore from the Gantry to the Stockyard at the Blast Furnace.

The Blast Furnaces

The main items of equipment were of course, the three Blast Furnaces, but the Department did not start or finish there. In fact they consisted of three main sections – as well as the Ore Handling Plant:

A. The Blast Furnaces,
B. The Gas Cleaning Plant,
C. Pig Casting Machine and Pig Stock bay, Mechanics and Electricians.

In the Blast Furnaces, when all three were in blast, they produced an average of 15,000 tons of iron per week and to do this about 30,000 tons of ore, 12,000 tons of coke, and 5,500 tons of limestone and dolomite were required. All of these materials were handled by the Ore Handling Plant and was not as straight forward as might appear at first sight. This was because, except for the coke, the materials were not received in a regular flow and also some nine or ten different grades of ore were used, each of which had to be treated as a separate commodity.

The largest individual consignments of ore were those from Labrador and Wabana, and the ports from which these ores were shipped were frozen for six months of the year. This accounted for the mountain of ore that could be seen from time to time from the Berry Edge Road, as it was necessary to take a year's supply of these ores in six months. Total ore stocks at any one time could amount to some 380,000 tons. Most of the ores were screened and the fines were blended with coke breeze and limestone dust and sintered to make a more suitable burden material. This sinter and the rough ore after screening, together with coke and fluxes (limestone and dolomite), formed the furnace burden. But it was not just a matter of charging the materials into the top of the furnace and hoping for the best. The charge had to be very carefully calculated, taking into consideration ore availability, chemical composition, physical state and cost.

For example, Wabana ore contained a high percentage of phosphorus, which adversely affected the iron. Conakry contained a high percentage of alumina, which would require extra fluxes and so increase the slag volume; but both these ores were comparatively cheap and readily available.

The Blast Furnace produced an average for each furnace of pig iron 750 tons, slag 350 tons, gas 80,000,000 cubic feet per day. Each furnace tapped about every four hours. The air or 'blast' compressed by blowers and heated in hot blast

A general view of the Blast Furnaces.

stoves to the desired controlled temperatures was passed through the hot blast mains and the tuyeres into the furnace. Here, it reacted with the incandescent coke to form carbon monoxide which has a strong affinity with oxygen at a high temperature and reduces the oxides of iron present in the ores to metallic iron. At the same time as the ore was being reduced the

Operations on No 3 Furnace.

limestone charged into the furnace, along with the ores and coke was calcined to lime which combined with the impurities of the ores to form a free running slag which lay on the top of the iron in the hearth. The slag was flushed from the hearth at regular intervals through the slag notches into self-dumping ladles.

Casting

Each furnace was cast according to a schedule, six times a day. The weight per cast averaged about 125 tons and the iron was run into 68 ton capacity hot metal ladles, in which it was either transferred to the mixer at the steelworks for open hearth plant operation (until 1964 when the Oxygen Steel Plant was commissioned, after which the iron was transferred to the L.D. vessels in the steelplant) or to the pig stranding machine.

On occasions it was necessary to cast some iron into pigs. This was done at the Pig Casting Machine. From the Pig Casting Machine, the iron was transferred to the Pig Stock Bay, where it was stockpiled until required either by the Melting Shop,

Tapping No 3 Blast Furnace.

the Foundry or for outside sale. In addition to iron, the furnaces produced two by-products, Blast Furnace gas and slag. The gas was a very useful substance, but on leaving the furnace it was laden with dust and before being passed to the Fuel Department for use in various parts of the Works, such as the Fell Coke Works and New Mill Soaking Pits, it was thoroughly cleaned. Cleaning was done at the Gas Cleaning Plant.

The dust so recovered was taken to the sinter plant and mixed in with the sinter blend and returned to the furnaces. From the dust catchers, the gas passed through the primary washing towers. After leaving the towers it went to the gas holder at the Fell Coke Works.

Slag, the other by-product, amounted to some 8,000 tons per week. It was disposed of on the slag tip where some of it was reclaimed for the manufacture of road ballast, etc.

Blast Mechanics

The main function of this department was to maintain the equipment used by the Blast Furnaces Production Department in the manufacture of iron. The major part of the work carried out was concerned with the four main sections of the plant. They were:

> Ore Handling Plant
> Sinter Plant
> Blast Furnaces and Pig Casting Machines
> Gas Cleaning Plant

When a furnace was 'blown in', it was expected to work night and day for many years. The need for really efficient maintenance was thus obvious, when it is realised that the complete overhaul of certain items can only be carried out during a relining operation. Small gas leaks at the furnace top could easily become serious if they were passed unnoticed. Equipment in use on a Blast Furnace were designed and constructed to last for a complete campaign – as the repair or replacement of certain components could be difficult, unpleasant and dangerous when the furnace was 'alive'.

It may be readily understood that close co-operation between the production and maintenance personnel was essential. Complete furnace overhauls were carried out by maintenance men, during which the blast mechanics undertook a large proportion of the work.

Changing pans on a Pig Casting Machine in the early 1960s.

J. Hornsby, C. Hill and J. Brewston changing pallets at the No 1 Sinter Plant.

Gas Plant maintenance was largely concerned with the upkeep of pumps, valves of all shapes and sizes, steam and compressed air services, settling ponds and filter plant.

Apart from the maintenance work, the work was extended in 1962 to include the erection and installation of equipment. This added to the already widely varied type of plant that the blast mechanics maintained. With such a large amount of plant continuously running, inspections had to form an important part of the work. The object was to keep the plant running efficiently in such a manner that production targets in output could be achieved. The maximum amount of maintenance that would restore the plant to the condition it was in when it was commissioned. This was neither economical nor necessary. On the other hand, the minimum amount of maintenance could result in serious breakdowns, causing large losses in production.

The optimum amount of maintenance existed somewhere between the two extremes and it was the duty of the blast mechanics supervisors and staff to determine those conditions when the plant would perform efficiently after several years of operation. This involved considerable amounts of clerical work and record keeping. Routine examinations were carried out throughout the plant and from these the necessary repair work was determined and carried out.

Blast Furnace Mechanics' annual dinner 1967.

J. Brennon and W. Wilkinson overhauling a main furnace redirecting water pump.

Mechanics E. Malpass, C. Malpass, D. Young and E. Tinkler.

The Wellman Slag Road Transporter was very nearly 100 tons in weight and could lift and transport waste slag from the Basic Oxygen Steel Plant at Consett.

The slag ladle, which itself weighed over 20 tons, was hoisted by two hydraulic rams on the transporter and hoisted piggy back style on to the back of the transporter. (See below.)

The liquid slag in the slag tub which contained many of the impurities from the steelmaking process is seen being emptied on to the slag heaps.

Care had to be taken in emptying the hot slag on to the ground, as any patches of rainwater could cause a chemical reaction and explosion.

When the slag tub had been emptied, it was hoisted back into position for further use in the steel plant. When cooled and treated, the graded slag was sold for roadstone throughout the United Kingdom.

Power Station

The first boiler was commissioned in August 1947, however it was not fully completed until 1949. The main plant consisted of 5 boilers with a maximum continuous output of 120,000 lbs per hour of steam. The distribution of power was controlled from a central control room, power generated being balanced with power brought in from the National Grid, the mix of power being arranged as far as possible to get power at its cheapest cost with reliability. During peak periods on the Grid system the Power Station met the full demand of the Works.

Above: R. Lynn racking in 11,000 volts, 600 amp switchboard.

Left: G. Bell and R. Gibson in the control room.

Below: P. Walton, A. Peacock and R. Mason on the operating floor of the boiler house.

PRODUCTION PLANNING DEPARTMENT, OPEN HEARTH STEEL PLANT & OXYGEN STEEL PLANT

J. Maddison, slab recorder, with trainer J. Harris and J. Welch completing slab card information. In the background is J. Walls, slide rule operator.

The Production Planning Office

The planning office was started on the 11th February 1953. The main functions were the planning production of all ingot, slab, plate, bloom and billet orders.

Plate Planning Section

Plate orders were issued in week and priority numbers by the Plate Sales Department in the Planning Office. These numbers indicated the order of priority and the week of the year in which the order had been planned for rolling. The Slab Providing Section received these orders and decided which was the most economical overall plate dimension to be rolled in the plate mill.

Mrs M. Thomson and Miss J. Thompson typing a rolling programme. A copy of the rolling programme was issued to the relevant departments concerned in the processing of an order to know the exact number of plates required and so a check could be made on the progress.

Ingot Providing Section

There were four ingot providers and four assistants in this section, and these men worked the 42 hour continuous working system. When the typist had transferred the information from the cards to the rolling programme, the cards and the copy of the rolling programme was passed to the ingot providing section. The assistant ingot provider sorted the cards into the various qualities of steel. There were 214 different specifications for steel, which could be rolled into plate. The ingot provider and his assistant then commenced planning ingots and casts of steel, completing one customer's order at a time and adhering to the rolling programme and priority numbers as far as possible. They checked the quality required and the rolling plate dimensions, thus they could determine the most suitable type of ingot required, to give an equally suitable slab, for rolling into the required plate dimensions.

When they had determined the analyses, the slab dimensions and the type of ingot required, they could inform the Steel Plant of the ingot requirements. The majority of ingots were 'tailor made', ie the ingot provider requested the

Steel Plant to teem the ingot to various heights down the mould to give the exact amount of steel required to finish the orders he had planned. There were five types of ingots normally planned for plates. These ingots varied in weight from 10 tons to 26 tons. Whilst planning these ingots, the Ingot Providing Sections aim was to have a total weight of approximately 78 tons for each ladle.

W. Jackson, Ingot Provider, and assistant John Dettmer preparing cutting sheets for slab shears.

Every morning an estimated tapping time programme was issued from the Steel Plant, from which the ingot provider proceeded to give the slab shears stocktaker in the Slabbing Mill full details of the dimensions required from each ingot. The documents used for giving this information were called cutting sheets and four copies were sent to the slab shears. The ingot provider or assistant had to try and assess how the slabs would be piled in the Slabbing Mill, so that the oldest orders were at the top of the pile, thus ensuring that those slabs were rolled at Hownsgill.

Approximately 100 ingots, yielding approximately 400 slabs, were planned for the Plate Mill each day.

A. Walton, Slab Provider, with assistant W. Burleigh and W. Allison, planning plate dimensions for Hownsgill.

Open Hearth Steel Plant (OHSP)

The Melting Shop, as it was known, was built prior to July 1925, replacing the three old melting shops, and coming into production on 75-ton acid furnaces. Very shortly afterwards basic furnaces were built. Even at this time Consett was keen to develop and in 1929 the 'B' furnace was built to an Italian design. The melting shop remained fairly static until about 1946 when a very ambitious and successful scheme was put into operation; to increase the furnaces up to 150 tons nominal capacity and, in addition, to convert from gas firing to liquid fuel and coke oven gas firing.

In 1950 the 'J' was built. Due to increased demand for steel and the building of the Slab, Blooming and Billet Mill, it was decided to boost the output from the modest 12/13,000 tons per week up to 20,000 tons plus. The tools provided for this job were two 25 ton acid Bessemer converters and in January 1954, Consett Iron Company was first to use the duplex process in Great Britain. It was a great tribute to the Open Hearth Plant and the Bessemer Plant that this was achieved.

In early 1954 trials were carried out using oxygen enrichment, the oxygen being supplied by a small satellite plant. The results of these trials were an encouraging 14% increased production. One of the first tonnage Oxygen plants in the country was built by B.O.C. to supply oxygen for this process.

In 1959 experimental work began with roof lancing which, after the closure of the Bessemer Plant in 1961, was adopted as standard practice. The record charge time using roof lances was 3 hours 10 minutes commence charge to tap. These lances did in fact give the ability to produce plus 20,000 tons per week without using the duplex process and put Consett in the front line of development.

Saturday, 6th May 1961 – A record breaking day on the 'L' furnace of the Open Hearth Steel Plant. First hand, Bob Wilson, broke the shop's top record by 20 minutes. Left to right: Bob Wilson, Ron Crocker, Bob Purvis and E. Amos.

The new Melting Shop at Consett as it appeared in 1925. The first cast was teemed on 2nd July of that year.

The Open Hearth Steel Plant's best year was 1960, when it averaged 19,800 tons per week and gave the record weekly total of 22,333 tons. Many thousands of tons of special steels were made in this plant. The last tap in the Open Hearth Steel Plant was in the early hours of the 31st December 1965, when production was transferred to the Oxygen Steel Making Plant.

'B' Furnace crew feeding fluorspar to the Open Hearth Steel Plant.

The L.D. Oxygen Steel Making Plant

The primary function of the Steel Plant was to make steel of the types and specification ordered by the customer. For as long as one can remember Consett had been classed as a 'jobbing steelmaker' supplying a wide and varied market. The Steel Plant operatives, from Plant manager to humble labourer, had to learn to be versatile and produce a wide range of steels. The 'make', or variety of types of steel could vary from plate steel for shipbuilding to rimming steel for the motor car industry, from high carbon steel for wire drawing to 9% nickel steel for low temperature pressure vessels.

Inevitably such variations resulted in challenges in a variety of ways, from change of work practice and methodology to quality assurance and control and assessing the finished product was both to customer standards and suitable for the requirement intended.

This was successfully achieved and made the steelmaker of Consett a specialist in every sense of the word and probably the most versatile operator in the country.

The L.D. Plant

The plant was commissioned in February 1964, and by December 1965 it was possible to close down the Open Hearth Shop and make all the steel in the new plant. The potential of the plant by 1968 was 1,000,000 tonnes per year, produced by two 130-ton L.D. vessels (the N. and P respectively, where one L.D. operated whilst the other was under repair), whilst another, No 3 (the 'S' vessel) was commissioned a little later in that year.

Later still, a fourth L.D. (the T. vessel, was commissioned about 1973, when No 2 was decommissioned).

The plant itself covered an area of approximately 32,750 square yards and was split up into four bays – charging, converter, casting and stripping bays and, slightly external to the main building, the Block Making Plant.

As a matter of interest, the letters 'L.D.' stand for the two towns in Austria, Lintz and Donowitz, where the process was invented and developed. Before actually describing the process itself, it is necessary to first consider the raw materials required for producing 130 tons of steel in 48 minutes.

Hot Metal Or
Blast Furnace Iron

Hot metal produced by the reduction of iron ore in the Blast Furnaces contained the pure iron which made steel, but in addition, it also contained impurities which had to be removed before steel could be made, namely carbon, silicon, sulphur and phosphorus. An average hot metal analysis is

W. Rigby (raw materials attendant) sampling a wagon of lime on arrival.

4.4% carbon, 1.0 % silicon, 0.04% sulphur, 0.15% phosphorus and 0.5% manganese.

When making a steel for rolling into plate the required analysis of the steel was of the order of 0.2% carbon, 0.03% silicon, 0.03% sulphur and phosphorus and 0.7% manganese. One can easily see from the two analyses the amount of impurities which had to be removed. The temperature of the hot metal was, on average, 1,280 deg C. to 1,300 deg C. whilst the temperature required for casting steel was 1,620 deg C. a rise of approximately 320 deg C.

Scrap

This had roughly the same analysis as the steel produced and did not contain any large quantities of impurities such as phosphorus, silicon and sulphur. The type of scrap used was very important as it effected the speed of working. Scrap coming from the Primary Mill was high in bulk density and could be quickly charged. Should there be a need to use merchant or bought scrap then that, being lighter, took longer to charge.

Lime

Limestone as we are all aware, occurs naturally. Lime was made by quarrying the stone and heating it in kilns until all the carbon dioxide was driven off. For L.D. steelmaking the quality of the lime had to be first class; it had to be burnt to the degree, not under burnt with still limestone in as that tended to make slag formation difficult and not over burnt as this made the lime less reactive with the same difficulty of slag formation. The sulphur content had to be low or this would increase the finished sulphur content of the steel, which had to be as low as possible.

Fluorspar

This material was charged with the lime and had the effect of fluxing the lime, ie making it go into solution to form a slag. Fluorspar was mined locally at Blanchland and in Weardale. In its mined condition (before crushing) it was in the form of white crystals tinged with blue, purple and orange.

Crushed Firebrick

This was produced by Consett's own brickworks from recovered waste material. It was charged with the lime and had the same effect, ie it fluxed the lime and made a slag.

Charging Boxes filled with scrap being received by steel plant scrap attendant Herbie Tinnion.

Oxygen

Should anyone ask, 'Which factor or invention made the biggest impact on the steel industry in the last 40 years?' then undoubtedly the answer would be, the advent of commercial oxygen which could be produced at a price which made its application to steelmaking an economical proposition. Commercial oxygen was produced by using a very cheap raw material – the air we breathe. Most of us remember from our school days that air contains approximately four parts of nitrogen and one part oxygen. This air was cooled under pressure until it liquified. Once this state had been reached then the oxygen and nitrogen were easily separated as each had different boiling points. The oxygen received from the British Oxygen Company had a purity of 99.5%.

G. Hogg (raw materials attendant) raking lime into the ground reception bunkers.

The L.D. Process

To fully understand the production of steel by the L.D. process, one has to have a little elementary knowledge of chemistry. Hot metal was received from the Blast Furnaces at an average temperature of 1290 deg C. When making an ordinary type of steel for rolling into plate there were two objects to achieve. To raise the temperature to 1620 deg C. (the temperature required to be able to 'teem' or 'cast steel' and to reduce the impurities to the required level.

How was this done? The impurities were removed by a process known as 'oxidation', which simply means the chemical combination of a substance with oxygen to form another substance or a gas. Consider each impurity which had to be removed. Carbon combined with the oxygen to form the gases carbon monoxide and carbon dioxide. The carbon monoxide burned inside and at the mouth of the converter and the heat thus generated was used for producing steam by means of the waste heat boiler. The silicon combined with the oxygen forming a substance known as 'silica', which in turn combined with the lime which had been added to make a slag to form a substance known as 'calcium disilicate' and here it remained never to return to the steel. The phosphorus combined with the oxygen to form a substance called 'phosphorus pentoxide', which in turn combined with the lime in the slag to form calcium triphosphate. Some of the sulphur combined with the oxygen to form a gas, sulphur dioxide, which escaped with the other gases, but most of it combined with the lime in the slag to form calcium sulphide.

The importance of a good lime and therefore a good slag in L.D. steelmaking may be readily understood. So much for the impurities; now, where do we get the heat from to raise the temperature from 1290 deg C. to 1620 deg C.? The important thing to remember is that oxygen is not a fuel in itself; the fuel is the impurities in the iron and heat is released when these burn with the oxygen in the air.

Making A Heat Of Steel

We have just tapped a high carbon heat, the vessel is empty and raring to go. The first operator has already ordered 100 tons of hot metal, 40 tons of scrap, 11 tons of lime, $1/2$ ton of firebrick and a $1/4$ ton of fluorspar. The hot metal was hung up on the charging crane, the lime, firebrick and fluorspar are ready in the weigh batch hoppers; along comes the scrap charging machine, its siren screaming out a warning of travel. The driver carefully positions it in front of the converter (which is tilted at about 35 degrees from the vertical) and within a minute 40 tons of scrap are dumped into the converter and the driver of the 160-ton charging crane pours the 100 tons of hot metal into the converter, the converter is swung up into the vertical position and we are ready to blow. The second operator lowers the lance into the vessel until it is 4 ft 6 in above the level of the liquid bath; oxygen is switched on and blown on to the bath at a rate of 10,000 cubic ft or 830 lbs per minute.

With a roar and belch of fume and flame from the vessel mouth, ignition between the oxygen and the metal takes place. The first operator signals to the fourth operator to start feeding the lime, firebrick and fluorspar (this takes 7-8 minutes). During this period the first operator carefully watches the mouth of the converter, at first the flame is not very bright as silicon is the first impurity to be removed. After about ten minutes the luminosity of the flame significantly increases, indicating that carbon is being rapidly removed. At the same time droplets of slag are being ejected from the converter mouth, proving we have a good slag.

Now is the time to push the process along faster and the oxygen flow rate is increased to 12,000 cubic ft or 1,000 lbs per minute. During this time the third operator is busily preparing the alloys required to be added to the steel to meet the customers needs.

The first operator continues to watch the flame at the converter mouth. He must be sure that his slag does not get too dry, for if it this happens, the phosphorous and sulphur will not be removed to the required level.

Conversely he must ensure that his slag does not become too fluid, causing heavy ejections from the vessel mouth and resulting in a poor yield. Generally speaking, to counteract a dry slag, he will increase the distance between the end of the lance and the bath level by raising the oxygen lance, and for a slag that is too fluid, decrease the distance.

We have been blowing now for 22 minutes; the flame at the converter mouth is not so bright and its edges are tinged with brown, indicating that the majority of the carbon has been

Forty tons of scrap being charged into the vessel by the scrap charging machine.

removed. The first operator signals for the lance to be removed. When this is done the vessel is carefully tilted to the horizontal position (the mouth of the vessel facing east). Samples of steel and slag are taken and quickly dispatched to the laboratory for analysis. One of the operators takes the temperature of the steel by immersing a pyrometer into the liquid bath. The temperature is 1630 deg C., ten degrees too hot to tap, but as we have to wait six or seven minutes for the results from the laboratory it will probably be 1620 deg C. by the time we are ready for tapping.

Hot metal from the blast furnace being charged into the vessel.

Everything depends now on the results of the samples; tension mounts as the crew waits.

The telephone rings, the fourth operator writes down the analysis; carbon 0.12%, sulphur 0.03% phosphorus 0.010% and manganese 0.18%. Quickly the first operator calculates the amount of alloys and coal required to add to the ladle to meet the specification. The boxes containing the alloys are placed over the chutes on the tapping side, the ladle car is driven into position and

Fergie Tait and Bob Robinson take a sample of steel.

the vessel tilted over on to the west side and the steel runs out of the taphole into the ladle. The first operator watches the ladle carefully and when it is approximately a quarter full instructs the third operator to add the alloys. When all the steel has run out of the converter, 3-4 tons of slag are allowed to run through the taphole on to the top of the ladle to act as an insulator. The vessel is then swung over to the east side and the slag poured into a slag ladle. The steel ladle is transferred by steel ladle car into the Casting Bay and picked up by the 180-ton casting crane. We look at the clock; it has taken us 48 minutes to produce 130 tons of steel.

Harry Carr taking and checking the temperature with a 'tem-tip'.

Ernie Telford weighing out alloys to be added to the steel as it runs into the ladle.

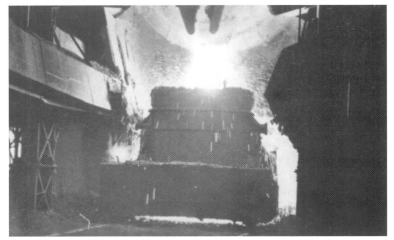

Steel being run out of the taphole into the steel ladle. The alloys were added to the ladle via the two chutes.

The Casting Of Steel

Whilst it is important to make the steel in the vessel to the correct specification, it is equally important for the production of sound products that the steel was correctly teemed or poured into ingot form. This process took place in the Casting Bay.

Left: End of tap – 130 tons of steel being lifted across to the Casting Bay for teeming.

Teeming

The process of pouring the metal from the ladle into a mould was known as 'teeming'. The moulds were placed upon pallets, which in turn were set upon bogies. The steel left the ladle via a nozzle controlled by a stopper rod. The size of the nozzle depended upon the quality of steel being

W. Robinson (Casting Bay), R. Nixon and W. Creegan during teeming.

teemed. The metal emitted from the nozzle had to flow in a vertical direction without any spray or slant.

Cast Preparation

The setting up of casts, ie the placing of moulds upon the pallet, was supervised by the Stripping Bay chargehand. This man was also responsible for the correct stripping times of all casts. He had to maintain close liaison with the Production Planning office to ensure that the right types of moulds were ready for a given time.

Ladle Preparation

The ladles were lined with fireclay bricks. The stopper rod inside the ladle consisted of firebrick sleeves which were threaded on to a cast iron bar. The nozzle of the ladle was fitted externally by one of three ladlemen and the rod fitted into the nozzle from the inside. The satisfactory production of good ingots required a meticulous approach by all concerned. Consideration had to be given to the end product of the steel so that necessary precautions could be taken during casting. The Steel Plant utilised all methods of ingot production, resulting in great versatility of the Casting and Stripping Bay personnel.

W. Bellamy setting the stopper in a ladle.

Jimmy McCusker preparing a cast.

W. Thompson and A. Harris supervising the setting of a cast before teeming.

J. Fox driving the stripper crane, removing moulds from ingots prior to despatch to the Primary Mill.

Steel Plant Engineers

The primary function of this department was to overhaul and maintain the plant and equipment to such a standard that steel production could proceed with minimum interruption.

E. Sullivan, (steel plant engineer), T. Brown (chargehand fitter), M. Healey (rigger) and M. Duffy (mate) changing a L.D. Oxygen lance.

SLAB, BLOOMING & BILLET MILL, OLD PLATE MILL & HOWNSGILL PLATE MILL

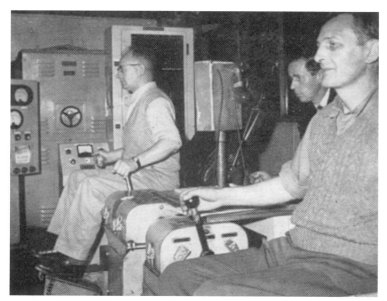

Left to right: R. Walker (screwer), R. Lowes (observer TRD) and R. Nichol (manipulator operator) in Slabbing Mill pulpit.

Slab, Blooming And Billet Mill

Even the natives of Consett found it difficult to remember what that area of the Works had looked like before the first part of the vast development scheme started. Landmarks known as the Office Bank and the Hall Road disappeared and in their place stood imposing buildings such as the Power Station, Bessemer Plant and the New Mill. To make possible the installation of the Mill in such close proximity to the Melting Shop, thus keeping track times to a minimum and at the same time avoiding any interference with the working of the Plate Mill and the Angle Mills, it was decided that the best layout of the Mill called for the bridging of the passenger and goods line of British Railways. This ran through a 200-foot long reinforced concrete tunnel and under the Mill floor at this point was carried on a 200-foot long steel bridge over the tunnel. So much for the site preparation. The Slab, Blooming and Billet Mills – a bright, clean and modern department which was justifiably the pride of the firm at the time.

Diversity Of Products

The Mills were laid down to produce slabs for re-rolling in the Plate Mills, slabs and blooms for sale, small slabs and billets for serving the Strip and Small Section Mill at Jarrow, and for sale.

From the large tonnages of small slabs and billets sent to Jarrow and to outside customers, a diversity of products were finally produced, eg rims for motor car wheels, car springs, telephone and fencing wire, welding rods, window frames, nails, harrow discs for farming implements and many others which we meet in everyday life.

A familiar sight to us all were the articulated tractors and trailers which transported a large proportion of the billets from the Mill to Jarrow and other places. Transport played a large part in a high production unit such as the Billet Mill when the clearing of rolled steel from the bays was of prime importance; not an enviable task in mid-winter, but a job well done.

One of the difficulties of working a combined Slabbing and Blooming Mill was making sure that the correct quality of steel, in the right type of ingot, was available for the particular shift being worked. The arrangement was for billets to be rolled on the 6-2 and 2-10 shifts and slabs for the Plate Mills on the 10-6 shift. To cope with

Blooming entering Roughing Mill.

H. Carr and L. Hall slinging hot slabs from piles, Slabbing Mill.

the situation was the Planning Department, whose task it was to order the steel from the Melting Shop to suit the orders presented to them by the Sales Department and to ensure that an adequate supply of ingots was available for the Mill.

Planning and executing the Mill programme which included many different qualities of steel and numerous sizes of slabs, blooms and billets, called for very close co-operation between all the departments concerned.

W. Grigg, slinging billets for Dispatch Loading Bay.

Record Outputs

It was interesting to note that with an almost identical number of men, the Mill could produce and despatch in one day of three shifts almost as much steel as the Angle Mill in one week working seventeen shifts. This gives some idea of the progress that had been made in Mill development over those years, future development included a battery of electric soaking pits.

The men on the production line were specialists in their own right. Years of experience gave them the ability, which became inborn, to handle the red-hot steel and to work it to fractions of inches. They were constantly in touch with each other over an inter-comm system and they worked as a production team.

The Mill rolled a million ingot tons a year and day by day the men on the machines saw to it that the flow was maintained to meet requirements. The re-heating of ingots to rolling temperature and the men who were in charge of the primary rolling of ingot. From the Cogging or Primary Mill the rolling passed to the shears where it was cut into lengths suitable to customers' requirements. If slabs were being rolled for plate they were taken off the Mill at the slab transfer bank after being through the shears.

Slabbing, Blooming And Billet Mill Millwrights

As with the maintenance men in the Plate Mill so it was with the millwrights in the Slabbing, Blooming and Billet Mill.

Many months before the holidays, Mr Vic Dent, Mill Engineer, and Mr Arthur Stokoe, his assistant, planned a programme of work to be done. Some of the jobs they had in mind were too big to be tackled during the normal maintenance periods. The work was scheduled and all parts ordered and

Junior 'Ops' relaxing after an outing in Weardale as part of their training.

prepared in readiness for the closure. The preparatory work was most important as it ensured adherence to the strict time-table for the fortnight.

When zero hour came, for the Mill men it was 'stop', but for the millwrights it was 'go'. And go they did, with all their skill and craftsmanship. It was 'all hands on deck' and the Mill became a hive of intense activity. Dismantling and stripping the machinery started the actual work programme and it was then that the men often found more work than had been anticipated.

But they knew their jobs and their satisfaction was when the Mill started up again and everything went according to plan. That was all the praise they needed.

The Origins Of The Plate Mills

Rolling Mills owe their inception to two innovations of the nineteenth century, the railroads and the iron-clad ships. In the beginning, plates were produced by a process we have all heard about which was known as 'puddling'. This very roughly meant heating the metal into plastic mass and literally beating it into sheets. Demand of course soon outstripped supply and eventually four mills were laid down at Consett to roll plates. These were the 'old mills' and as they were the product of early rolling development, they too soon became obsolete. By the time they had coped with the First World War they were not only obsolete but no longer an economic proposition and certainly incapable of dealing with the vastly increased demand. And so it was decided to re-construct and lay down two more modern mills in 1925 capable of rolling between them most types of steel plate from the types of steel plate from the range then in demand in the North East.

The Plate Mill in 1925.

Development

In 1952 two continuous type furnaces were put into operation to replace the batch furnaces and the (then newly constructed Slab, Bloom and Billet Mill) took over the job of providing the Plate Mill with slabs from their own Mill.

The Plate Mill ceased production of the slabs and was dismantled and the site was cleared for the erection of a new foundry. The new continuous furnaces were fed from the rear with cold slabs pushed forward by depilers. These slabs were pushed, one behind the other, and as they progressed further

Plate Mill veterans' annual dinner in 1967.

into the furnace they were subjected to higher and higher temperatures until rolling temperature was reached. The simple principle being that as each cold slab was pushed in, it ejected a slab from the front ready to roll.

Plate steel from these two mills serviced the Second World War. It was said that they had the pleasure of seeing a 500 kilo bomb bounce off the armour plating made at Consett on the deck of a famous battleship at Scapa Flow!

Steel for shipbuilding; containers for Atomic reactors; storage tanks; gas-holders; bridges and locomotives it was all made in these two mills, known colloquially as the 'heavy end' and the 'light end.

When these mills were made redundant, after the new Hownsgill Plate Mill was commissioned in April 1961, they were used for the purposes of storage and car parking until the closure of the Works in 1980.

Hownsgill Plate Mill

Hownsgill Plate Mill was one of the most modern steel-rolling mills in Europe, capable of producing plain plates and floor plates quicker and more accurately and with a surface quality not before achieved at Consett. It was the first 4 high floor plate mill in the country, plates from which were exported to many countries. The slab bay, which received finished steel slab from the Slab, Blooming and Billet Mill by rail, stocked the slabs. As per customer requirement, the slabs were 'charged' by crane into the soaking pits for reheating prior to rolling to size.

Nos 1 & 2 Hot Banks which allowed rolled hot steel plates to cool before marking up, sheering to required size and then despatch to customer.

A view of the Slabyard.

Stainless Steel Plates

In addition to normal steels at Hownsgill, a certain amount of hire-rolling was carried out on stainless steel. In the week ended 1st March 1970 the Mill produced 10,907 tonnes of finished plate. In addition to the normal plate mill finishing processes, facilities included pressure quenching, normalising and tempering furnaces and shot blasting. This enabled the processing of a greater variety of high price special steels for advanced engineering purposes. Plate Order Planning and Slab Planning was carried out against a computerised programme. Hownsgill Plate Mill closed in November 1979.

Maintenance Shops

A large amount of work was necessary to keep the structures of various sections of plant in workable condition. There were three plating squads to handle that side of the business. The squads were led by W. Frosdick, F. Coulson and W. Dower. There were hundreds of guards and grids which needed constant attention and repair and these squads were fully stretched to keep the job going. The maintenance shops were equipped to deal with most

Hownsgill Gentlemen's Club – Annual functions showed how many people, their friends and families enjoyed a night out.

day-day maintenance jobs and anything outside the range was sent to the central Maintenance Shops. The equipment in the shop included two Lang lathes, one 54 circular grinder, one shaper, one milling machine, one 60-inch vertical borer, one radial arms driller and the usual small grinders, etc. The work in the shop was supervised by Mr R.A. Strand, dayshift foreman, and was covered by the shift foreman outside dayshift hours. The shift foremen were Messrs D.L. Gibb; A.H. Newton; R.S. Ramshaw and J.E. Winter, who covered a large area and a great deal of complicated equipment.

Stan Hogg and Norman Sheldon working on the controls of No 3 maintenance crane.

Electrical Section

Mr H. Jones (mechanical) and Mr J. Mutch (electrical) assisted in the general engineering of the plant, each taking charge of his own particular section. As the smooth running of a department called for a large number of records so that any frequent failures of any particular unit could be highlighted, the amount of work involved was very substantial.

The records and the weekly summaries of delays along with the planned record cards were very ably dealt with by Miss B. Johnson, the Mill Engineer's secretary, who could usually manage to produce the required information when it was needed.

Mr J. Davison was also assisting and one of his jobs was to organise the gigantic task of meeting the requirements of H.M. Inspector of Factories with regard to guards and safety appliances.

The centre of operations in the Hownsgill Mill with regard to the electrical equipment was undoubtedly the motor room with its high and low tension distribution gear, generating sets, control panels and the twin motors driving the 4 high plate mill.

There were two sources of electrical supply for the Mill. Normally the power required was drawn from the 132,000 volt grid whose pylons provided the area a new landmark in the Consett area. This power was transformed at the new electricity board sub-station at Templetown to 11,000 volts at which pressure it was supplied to the Plate Mill. The other supply was also at 11,000 volts and came from the Company's own power station, in the event of a grid failure could maintain essential services at Hownsgill.

A large part of the electricians' work in this Mill as in others entailed repair and maintenance of the 15 production and 6 maintenance cranes. The duties of the cranes were arduous and continuous and care was required during overhaul periods to ensure their maximum efficiency was available at all times.

A great deal of equipment in outlying sections was included in the maintenance lot of the Mill and these added up to quite a large quantity of electrical equipment for driving and controlling, eg pump houses, lighting and such items as traffic lights and the main gate.

The Mill electrical staff worked on a continuous shift system under charge hand J. Wills, A. Willis, R. Sanderson and F. Morgan, each with a motor house attendant and two electricians together with their mates. Major repairs and installations were carried out by dayshift squad of electricians, mates and apprentices under the direction of C. Cooper. He also provided holiday and sickness relief personnel for the various shifts so that these never became understaffed.

Hownsgill Engineers, The Annual Holiday Shutdown

The Works' holidays meant just the opposite for the Company's maintenance staffs. It meant two weeks' of concentrated endeavour to service machinery so that when the holidays were over the production belt would work smoothly. In the Mills in particular the workmen looked forward to a fortnight away from work hardly had their coats on when the engineers took over.

Covers came off and in a short time the machinery was stripped down. A programme was laid down for the work to be done in the period. That embraced all classes of maintenance men whose job at Hownsgill Plate Mill was to service the machinery and electrical installations in their care.

A visitor to the Mill in the middle of the holidays would have been astounded and he or she could be forgiven for wondering if ever it would all be put together again. But the men engaged on the major overall were experts in their own field and they were aware of their responsibilities and also – which was most important – the time factor. Mr M. Hepworth, the Company's Plate Mill Engineer and his men saw to it that everything was in working order on the shift when the Mill began rolling again.

Hownsgill 2nd Annual Leek Show, 1967.

SECTION FIVE

FELL COKE WORKS, SPIRACON DEPARTMENT, TEMPLETOWN SILICA BRICK PLANT & DELVES FIREBRICK WORKS

Kiln setters – J. Crawley, D. Tathons, F. Richardson and R. Douglas.

The Fell Coke Works

In 1924, when Mr E.J. George (later Sir E.J. George) was general manager, the first battery of all silica coke ovens ever built in Europe was put to work at the Fell Coke Works. Part of this battery of 60 ovens was put out of service in December 1954, to allow for the building of new and more modern ovens, while the remaining ovens continued in operation until January 1965, having carbonised more than 170,000 tons of coal per oven. The silica bricks and shapes for this battery of 60 ovens were made at Templetown Brickworks between the years of 1921-24 when Mr A.H. Middleton (later Dr A.H.

A coke oven in operation.

Middleton) was the manager of the Coke and Brickworks departments and the engineer in charge of the new silica brickworks was Mr H. Boot, who became Managing Director of Consett Iron Company during the late 1940s.

J. Railton and H. Pearson cleaning a door frame in the Coke Works.

Spiracon Department

Spiracon was the registered trade name for the spirally welded steel pipe produced by the Constructional Department of Consett Iron Co Ltd one of Britain's major steel producing companies.

E. McKinnel (burner) cutting 16-inch pipe to length on the '1,000' pipe machine.

W. Elliot (left, machinist) and T. Askew (slinger) setting pipe into bending and levelling machine.

Templetown Silica Brick Plant

At one time this plant was the largest unit in the country producing Silica shapes for the carbonising industries, as well as bricks and blocks for steelworks and for the glass and other industries. The output capacity of the plant was 500 tons per week of shapes, 200 tons of bricks and blocks and about 150 tons of cements for various purposes. All the raw material ganister was historically drawn from the Company's own quarries.

A. Barron, A.T. Telford and W. McNally on No 2 Brick Press.

Delves Firebrick Works

The original plant was put into operation in 1864 and was worked in conjunction with Beehive Coke Ovens, the waste heat from which was used for brick drying and burning. The raw material, seggar clay, was obtained from local collieries and also from open-cast workings for manufacture into Fireclay Refractories for Steelworks, Blast Furnaces and Gasworks. The equipment consisted of two Grinding Mills, Pug Mills, De-Airing Machines and Presses, together with two Brick Making Machines for squares. The drying was carried out on two large drying floors capable of being sectionally heated and firing was done in coal-fired Belgian and Dunnachie Kilns. The output capacity of the plant was about 17,500 tons per year.

Templetown annual dinner in the 1960s.

ANCILLARY ENGINEERING DEPARTMENTS

Blacksmiths, Boiler Shops, Engine Sheds, Pattern Shops, Fitting and Machine Shops, the Foundry and Training Centre

Bill Lewins being presented with wedding presents with Engine Sheds' personnel in attendance.

Blacksmiths' Shop

The Blacksmiths' Shop was one of the oldest established departments in the Consett Iron Company, yet how many workers realised what an important job it played in the maintenance of the integrated Iron and Steelworks at Consett? The Blacksmiths' Shop supplied all forgings up to two tons which were required for the plant. Anything from a cotter-pin to a roller shaft 11 inches in diameter by 15 feet long.

Before the 1924 reconstruction of the Works, there had been four Blacksmiths' Shops situated in different parts of the Works. Of these, only one could boast of having a mechanical hammer, whereas the other shops still worked in the traditional style of every job being started and finished on the anvil, with the striker swinging his 10 lb or 14 lb hammer. Drawing out, cutting, bending and welding were all done by hand. In those days it was quite commonplace to see three strikers hammering at a white-hot bar with perfect timing and the smith's hand hammer flashing at alternate blows, signifying where the next blow should be struck.

During the reconstruction the Blacksmiths' Shop was one of three maintenance departments which was moved away from the centre of the Works and built near the northern boundary of the plant. The idea was to make a modern shop with better facilities and by moving the shop nearer to the boundary it gave more valuable space in the centre of the Works for further expansion of the production departments.

The new shop was vastly different from the old types, for it was equipped with three pneumatic hammers with capacities of 3, 7$^1/_2$ and 20 cwt respectively and serviced with four wall jib cranes. There were two coal-fired furnaces and 14 coal-fired smith's hearths.

From 1947, the Blacksmiths' Shop had many further developments, with increased pneumatic hammers to five, five swing jib wall cranes; a 100 ton horizontal press; an electric flash butt welding machine; a cold saw; and a Shorter hardening machine. They then introduced 10 coke oven gas-fired furnaces of various capacities and four coal-fired smith's hearths.

Practically all of the blooms, billets and rounds used in the shop were rolled by the mills at Consett and Jarrow. The exception was when orders quoted a special alloy steel to be used and then the material had to be ordered from outside.

W. Collins (foreman) forging a 20 cwt Pilkington Pneumatic hammer.

Boiler Shops

Situated at the north end of the Works on a site which was part of the old Tin Mills was the Boiler Shop. The name being somewhat of a misnomer with the disappearance of steam locomotion, boilers became a rarity. Primarily, the Boiler Shop was a maintenance department responsible for the renewal or repair of steel fabrications worn in service. The Boiler Shop was well equipped both with men and machines to also supply a considerable amount of the new steelwork then required in the Works, be it as a length gas main or a complete steel furnace.

The Boiler Shop comprised of two bays each with a 10-ton overhead cranes. The first bay being used for plate preparation and containing the plate edge plane, levelling machine, plate bending machines, guillotine, drilling machines and profile burning machines. Whilst in the other bay were the bar straightening machine, punch and cropper and a second battery of drilling machines. This bay was used as an erection bay.

All orders were routed to the Boiler Shops via the shop's office. The first action was to arrange for the supply of the necessary material, either from their own stock and from the Steel Stockyard, or to order through the Buying Department plates from the Plate Mill or sections from outside suppliers. Over 3,000 tons of material was allocated in this way each year.

Loaded as required on to trailers, this material was fed into the shop in proper sequence by means of an Auto-Shunter. This machine, which was basically a Fordson tractor, was capable of pulling 200 tons of loaded wagons, and was fitted with normal tractor rubber-tyred wheels, was able to manoeuvre on the proverbial sixpence.

Highly skilled craftsmen on the template floor, using wood, cardboard, template board, paper and sheet metal, prepared in advance the templates for each job. As some of this work involved complicated mathematical calculations, the apprentices found their period of training on the template floor a direct application of the knowledge gained at day or evening classes.

Platers and apprentices working with these templates or direct from drawing accurately, marked on each plate or section the shape required and the position of each of the holes. Oxy-propane burners moving from one job to another cut the steel to the shape previously marked by the platers while three longitudinal profiling machines cut the many and varied shapes required.

Profiling machines being operated by J. Millhouse, R. Wheatley and H. Losh.

Engine Sheds

The Engine Sheds by the very fact of its name and situation at Templetown, was perhaps considered by some people to be only a shed where locomotives were parked and a few minor repairs carried out. In point of fact, it was an essential and busy department, being a railway workshop in miniature and carrying out the same repairs in the same manner as much larger railway workshops, such as the Darlington or the Doncaster workshops.

At one time there were two running sheds, one for the steam locomotives and the other for the diesel, this having been built in the late 1950s to keep the two types of locos separate and also to house equipment applicable to these locos only. In addition to the above there were Fitting and Machine Bays, Welding Bay, Coppersmithing, Blacksmiths' Shop (complete with a drop hammer, paint shop, rope splicing etc). All manner of tradesmen were employed to enable the department to be self-contained to a great degree in its activities.

Early Days

The siting of the department in relationship to the main Works was perhaps influenced by the need to be reasonably central to both the iron and steelworks and the local collieries. The locomotives were maintained by the Engine Sheds from as far afield as Chopwell and Langley Park. The shops had, of course been expanded since the first building was erected and as new technologies prevailed. By 1958, there were 40 ton, 20 ton and 3 ton capacity electric overhead cranes, which were essential for the major overhauling of the large locomotives which were by then being operated. The first diesel loco of note to be put into operation was in 1947 and then another in 1949. By 1958 there were some 18 diesel locos in operation with another 20 steam locos at this time, 17 at Consett and three at Jarrow.

It is perhaps interesting to note that diesel No 9, which was of 300 hp capacity, was the first loco to be built by Consett Iron Company, was partly designed by them and completely built by the company at the Engine Sheds by their personnel (and justly proud of the fact too!) The diesel

No 9 – the first locomotive to be built by Consett Iron Company.

and electrical equipment and miscellaneous detail for this loco were purchased from outside sources, but all other details were made at the Engine Sheds.

A number of details which had been put into practice with this loco were incorporated in the new locos which were delivered from Hunslet Engine Co, Leeds.

An early Works locomotive – the original B9 in 1887. The crew are, left to right: John Reed, George Burdon and Will Lumsden (driver).

Another interesting feature was the 'fireless' loco which in turn was designed and built at the Engine Sheds. An orthodox steam loco (B14) 16 inch cylinder was the basis of this loco; the wheels in it were taken from an old steam crane E11 and, with cutting and building and modifying here and there, the 'fireless' loco then emerged. It was used as an experimental loco only.

Cranes

Everyone employed at the company recognised the old E class cranes, but perhaps are not aware that apart from being cranes they are museum pieces, by the fact that they existed no where other than at Consett. The oldest crane in operation in 1958, E1, was built in 1887 by Black Hawthorn was still going strong, although keeping the same in repair constituted a major headache for Engine Shed staff. There were still five of these cranes in operation in 1958.

The Engine Sheds' personnel were thus responsible for the maintenance of steam and diesel rail cranes, excavators, bulldozers, generators and Pollock ladles etc. In addition, all of the maintenance work was carried out for the (then Crookhall)

'E2' – Especially designed for the early Works and was still in use 70 years later (1957).

Foundry, including electric overhead cranes, hoists, sandmills, compressors, pneumatic tools, etc. Another important feature of the Engine Sheds' activities was the making and repair of brickmoulds for the

Engine Sheds and personnel pictured with a new diesel on its completion in the late 1950s.

Templetown and Jarrow Brickworks, a highly skilled section of the department.

By 1966 all of the steam locos at Consett had gone, with the sole exception of B 13 which was used at the Jarrow Works for steam raising purposes only. Two old steam cranes were still retained, Nos E1 and E9. The E1 had by then been converted from coal burning to oil burning and was still capable of doing excellent work re-railing etc.

Engine Sheds' annual dinner, January 1965.

Fabrication Department

Between the Tin Mill Road and Park Road (Consett Bank) at the northern extremity of the Consett Steelworks was a covered area of some 95,000 square feet. This comprised of an office block, workshops which comprised of six parallel bays each with an overhead travelling crane, as well as a Template Shop and Stores. The capacity of the cranes varied from $2^1/_2$ to 10 tons in the largest bay.

Alongside was an open stock gantry and two scotch derrick cranes which together covered some 40,000 square feet. That was the fabrication Department. As part of a Company employed in the production of iron and steel, this department specialised in the forming, shaping and joining of steel plates and sections and produced both simple and complex fabricated steelwork.

Unlike most departments of the Company, the fabrication department were consumers of steel although many of its products contributed to the manufacture of iron and steel.

The main raw materials were purchased from the Consett Plate Mills and the Jarrow Section Mills, whilst larger rolled steel sections were purchased from outside the Company.

Plates, rough cut to size, were conveyed by tractor and trailer to the stock gantry at the Fabrication Department and off-loaded with an over head travelling crane. These plates were transferred to the workshops by an electrically-driven rail bogie as and when required.

The Plate Stockyard showing crane and transfer bogie.

Marking Off – Stan Walton (plater) plucks the chalk line held by Eric Dawson whilst Harry Pigg (chargehand) stands by to check the results.

Steel sections were stocked in the steel stockyard (Stores Control) and conveyed to the workshops and saw benches by mobile crane. In order to appreciate fully the combined performance of the office and the workshops, it is perhaps best to separate the office work from the manual work, although it was a fact that the office was an integral part of the workshops. There was a staff of thirty two in the office. Once a delivery date had been quoted and confirmed it was important that separate and comprehensive records were kept of the amount of work on hand and for the future.

The prime plate materials were fed into the shops by means of an electrically transfer bogie and were moved from operation to operation by the overhead cranes. The steel sections were fed from outside saw benches into the shops by a diesel rail crane which passed through and along the end of each bay.

The operators in the shops were of three-grades namely skilled, semi-skilled and unskilled and the majority of craftsmen had served an apprenticeship of five years. The template makers were probably the most highly skilled craftsmen in the shops, for they were responsible for the calculation and laying down of developments as well as laying out and checking all dimensions. They made all wood and hardboard templates which were used on the shop floor and provided detailed sketches of the various items required for the make-up of a customer's requirements. The template floor was the beginning of all the more complicated structures. The platers were split into two sections: 'hand' and 'machine', as the type of work carried out by each section was literally by hand or by machine. The hand platers marked off at the early stages of each job and carried out all the assembly work for riveting, welding and bolting.

On some of the larger and more complicated structures it was necessary to erect the structure, in part or complete, to prove the fit-up and dimensions. This work was also carried out by the hand platers. The machine platers operated a variety of machine tools for the cutting, shaping, bending, forming and rolling of steel plate and steel sections. Guillotine and open shears were used for cutting plates whilst cropping machines were used for cutting sections. Heavy mangles were used for levelling plates, whilst bending rolls were used for the shaping of cylindrical and conical work.

Plates and sections were bent and formed into a variety of shapes on bending and folding machines as well as brake presses and hydraulic presses. Shaped and round holes were provided on punching machines. Burners operated a variety of machines which used oxygen and propane gas to burn through steel. Hand torches and small tracks were used for the straight forward burning, whilst special profile cutting machines cut practically any shape from a template. Large flame planing machines prepared the edges of plates for welding, all four edges of large plates were cut at the same time.

Welders and riveters were employed in the joining together of steel. The welders used electrodes for manual-arc welding, whilst the union-melt submerged arc welding was used for the heavier deposits. Riveting required a squad of at least three operators, the first to heat the rivets to make them soft, a second to hold the rivets in position and the third to knock down the heads with a hammer.

Planers operated two types of machine. Surface planing machines were used with cutting tools such that a good level surface could be obtained on steel over a large area, whilst edge planing machines were used for cutting a variety of preparations on the edges of plates or sections.

Drillers use a variety of machines, although all with the object of obtaining round holes. Radial drills were used for the drilling and tapping, whilst portable electrical or pneumatic drills were used for holes in awkward positions and for reaming out holes for fitted bolts and pins.

Other operators who helped with the fabrication of steel were the blacksmith with his fires, hammers and sets, the sawyers and the platers' helpers. The crane drivers, the slingers and the labourers kept the materials moving from operation to operation until finally the job was finished, except for inspection and painting or possibly shot blasting before painting. Every job presented its own problems. Therefore, to ensure that the crafts and experience of the many trades necessary to the fabrication of steelwork were not lost, a number of youths were apprenticed to be skilled craftsmen.

Drilling holes in foundation work – John Lee and Vincent Corr.

The Pattern Shop

Pattern Shop is a very misleading title for the many crafts which were represented in what was a versatile department. In addition to patternmaking, every aspect of plant maintenance was also carried out. It serviced every part of the plant, also the Fell Cokeworks, Templetown Works, Jarrow Mills and Brickworks and Weldments at Derwenthaugh. The organisation functioned under the control of Mr S. Unsworth, MIBF.

Patternmaking

This section, established about 1860, was one of the oldest in the Company and it was the birthplace of most machinery. Until the patternmaker began his work, the machine was merely a design on paper. He was the most highly skilled worker connected with his industry. He seldom, if ever, made the same type of thing twice and knowledge was always being acquired. In addition to working from very complicated mechanical drawings with nothing else to guide him, he had to have a thorough knowledge of other ancillary trades. He was an exalted craftsman the greatest common denominator as well as the least common multiple of industrial production. That patternmakers could be found in all kinds of administrative posts was due largely to their training in their craft.

Patterns were made for all classes of castings in cast steel, cast iron and non-ferrous metals ranging from the smallest bearings to all types of ingot moulds and slag ladles. Patterns were made for all methods of moulding, as required, for despatch to foundries in England, Scotland and Wales for castings which could not be produced in the old Foundry at Crookhall.

Painting

This section attended to the preservation and decoration of all buildings and structures, whether of wood, steel or brickwork, overhead cranes, gas holders, etc. Indeed, everything which required painting on the plant. Machine painting, wagon painting, paper-hanging and signwriting were also carried out. The far-reaching influence of the various colour schemes carried out, contributed in no small way to the establishment of happier labour relations and healthier, safety conditions on the plant, whilst the psychological influence had a profound effect on human moods and reactions. Repainting of the plant had to

Bob Robson, Bill Russell, Jack Hall and Clive Pooley making patterns for casting steel extension guides for the SBBM.

be carried out without interrupting production. This called for careful planning and the utmost co-operation and the closest liaison between Pattern Shop and departmental heads. Vacuum cleaners of all types were used to remove initial dust, etc and the latest types of equipment such as mechanical scrapers, pneumatic rollers and spray equipment was used to speed up work, relieve fatigue, and lessen cost. If certain painting work was let to outside contractors, the Pattern Shop ensured that it was carried out to full specification by daily inspection. On work involving specialised treatment, an advisory service was sometimes called

Neil Walton, Wally Lee, A. Griffiths and Jack Griffiths constructing sectional wood forms to form the profile for lining an experimental steelmaking vessel with dolomite. (Later developed into L.D. steel vessel.)

in for consultation. Specialised painting was carried out at the Garage, where all road transport vehicles such as tractors, trailer ambulances, mobile cranes, bulldozers, vans, etc were serviced by the Pattern Shop.

Eric Raine, Fred Wardle, Eddy Dodd, Cliff Capstick, H. Armstrong and Matt Hutton in the Joiners' Shop.

Pattern Shops

All patternmaking for steel, iron and brass castings as were required by the iron and steelworks, cokeworks and brickworks were carried out by this department.

Modern woodworking machinery, such as lathes, saws, planers and electrical driven small tools contributed greatly to the efficient production of patterns.

Tommy Lock, Bill Ferguson, Tom Pratt and Bob Lightfoot effecting repairs to roof glazing at the Engineering Shops.

A further activity was the production of wood moulds required by the Brickworks for brick making. In addition, all joinery, minor building repairs and painting etc, required by the Iron and Steelworks and ancillaries was carried out by squads of trained men from this department.

Fitting And Machine Shops

Most of the fitting and machine work entailed in the maintenance of the Iron and Steelworks was dealt with by this department comprising of three bays, a light machine bay, a heavy machine bay and an erection bay.

The light machine bay was serviced by numerous swing jib wall cranes of 15 cwt or 20 cwt capacities. A 10 ton electric overhead cranes serviced the heavy bay and a floor operated 10 ton electric overhead crane serviced the erection bay.

A small tool-room adjacent to the main buildings dealt with drill, tool and cutter grinding, jig making, etc, as required. Machines were installed primarily for their suitability in dealing with the varied work necessitated in the maintenance of the Iron and Steelworks. Planing, milling, slotting, shaping, horizontal and vertical boring, turning, gear cutting, grinding and drilling work could be carried out with ease.

The pressing on and off of wheels and rollers was carried out on a 300-ton capacity horizontal press of the Company's own design.

A further activity of this department was metal spraying. By the use of this method, hydraulic rams etc, could be sprayed with stainless or nickel steel as required. In addition, worn pump spindles, shafts, etc, could be brought up to size and re-used.

The finishing off of these rams, shafts and spindles was completed by grinding.

R. Chambers cutting worm wheels on a gear hobbing machine.

R. Bewley turning on a Ward's No 8 combination turret lathe.

The Foundry

The new foundry was put into production in July 1959, replacing the old Crookhall Foundry, and was built at the south end of the old Plate Mill on the site previously occupied by the Soaking pits for the old Cogging Mill. Founding was one of the oldest of the crafts and was a complex industry, which relied to a large extent on the human element. It involved all categories of labour, craftsmen, trained personnel for melting iron and bronze, sand preparation, dressing castings, and other graded process workers.

The Foundry was divided into three bays:

Cupola Bay, which housed cupolas and blower house mould drying stoves.

Heavy Bay, which was used for the production of ingot moulds, pallet plates, slag ladles, large jobbing castings, sand plant and dressing shop.

Light Bay, which was divided into sections, core shop light jobbing castings, brass and white metal shop, moulding, boxes and sand storage.

In addition there was an Amenity Block, comprising lock and shower rooms, toilets and dining hall.

Training Centre

For its size, the Company's Training Centre was one of the best equipped in the steel industry. Site preparation work started on 23rd January 1967, but well before then the need for a training centre for technicians, apprentices and operatives had become apparent. It was built to meet the needs of 'off-the-job' training to a specific syllabus. Those taking part received a thorough grounding in their subjects from fully qualified instructors. Building work on the 9,000 square ft area went well on schedule under the supervision of Mr Eric Oliver, Assistant Engineer-Development Department and his staff. There was accommodation for 80 young people. The facilities comprised of, main workshop, electric shop, two classrooms, dining room, staff offices, toilet and locker room, stores and heat treatment room.

The first intake of forty-five apprentices, four technical trainees, ten metallurgical technicians and one university student commenced their training on the scheduled date, 8th September 1967, with a one week Works' Induction Course. The engineering trade apprentices followed an integrated course (stage 1) for six months and this included twelve weeks fitting and turning, six weeks electricity and six weeks plating and welding. The second period of six months (stage 2) provided more specialised training for the individual trades. Patternmaker and moulder apprentices received their off the job training at Gateshead Technical College because the numbers involved did not warrant the equipment and instructors that would be required.

The building trade apprentices were grouped together with the technical trainees and metallurgical technicians for a three month course which covered one month each at fitting and turning, electrical and plating, and welding, this being considered a good introduction to apprenticeship by affording hand and eye co-ordination.

Each of the crafts followed a set syllabus of exercises which included progressive hand and tool operations supported by demonstrations and lectures given by the appropriate instructors.

The exercises, as far as possible, were confined to the making of tools and useful equipment, which the apprentices would retain. All results were assessed and recorded. Engineering drawing was an integral part of training and all apprentices spent two hours a week at the drawing board, under the supervision of Mr A. Hogarth, section leader, Maintenance Drawing Office.

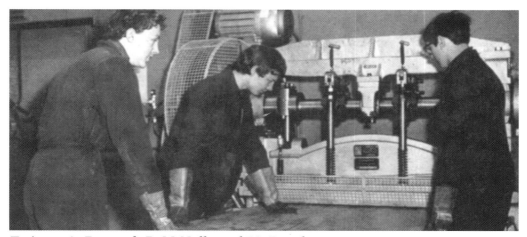

Trainees A. Barnard, B. McNally and M. Douglass.

Written craft and drawing examination papers were set every three months so that progress could be assessed. These were followed by a correction period when mistakes and omissions were rectified. Twelve Accident Prevention Lectures followed by an examination, were included in the first three months of the course, these were given by the safety Department. Log Book writing was another feature. Each trainee made a record of lectures and work done each week and this became his personal property on

Students and officials at Lambton Castle in November 1964.

conclusion of his training in the school. Since the trainees and building trade apprentices left in December, 1967, there had been eight second year fitters and turners, one plater, and one wagonwright in the school. These would return to their respective departments in April 1968, after a period of eighteen weeks and would be replaced by other second year boys.

The most advanced training given included repair and assembly of machines and equipment. For this they were well provided with a set of old levelling rolls from the Boiler Shop, a small compressor unit from the Development Department, a machine coolant pump, an old milling machine from the Fitting Shop and a small four stroke petrol engine and pieces of electrical equipment from a private donor.

Junior Operative Training

The Junior Operatives Training Scheme was introduced in January 1963, with the aim of providing comprehensive training for boys who would eventually be employed in the production departments of the Company. Applications for junior operative training were received from 16-year-olds and selection interviews were held in September of each year.

The interviews were held by the Junior Operative Advisory Committee, consisting of management and trade union representatives. Training began with a one-week course consisting of lectures on production, services, health and safety, Works visits and films. Following that the boys were placed in departments, where they were additional to normal staffing so that they were available for training.

Periods of three to six months were spent in each of the major production departments so that at the end of the training the junior operative would have a good working knowledge of the plant. Departments included in the training programme were: Fuel, Fell Cokeworks, Blast Furnaces, Slab Bloom and Billet Mill, Power Station, Steel Plant, Plate Mill, Stores Control and Traffic. Permanent appointments to a department were usually made after two to three years' training.

All junior operatives attended Consett Technical College on one day per week, where they took a course which had been specially designed for them. In addition, they attended classes on two evenings per week to take the City and Guilds iron and steel operatives' course and to receive instructions in accident prevention. Eventually they would progress to the new advanced courses for operatives, which had just been introduced.

Arthur Summerell and W. Leybourne rebuilding an air compressor unit.

A PATTERNMAKER'S STORY

by Bill Johnson

Now in retirement, after 33 years working in the newspaper industry – a far cry from patternmaking – my mind often takes me back to that period twenty years ago, when I watched with dismay the depressing TV news programmes announcing the possible closure of Consett Steel. At one time there was hope, for didn't I hear that the plant was making a profit? Then of course when the blow fell and the closure was announced my thoughts went out to those hardworking men and their families whose world must have been turned upside-down overnight. Then I thought of the number of young boys leaving school who would now be deprived of an apprenticeship and the opportunity to follow in their father's footsteps and to make a future for themselves. Not only that, but what of the skills and crafts that had now disappeared with such a closure, as well as the hopes and dreams of so many? Twenty years have passed since those dreadful days and I can only hope that life has been kinder, through time, for the people affected.

It was with mixed emotions that I left home at 7-30 one September morning in 1947. Walking down from Blackfyne, I found my mind mulling over the years of schooling that now lay behind me. What had I learnt? What did I know, at the age of sixteen? Very little about working for a living, that was certain and yet, here I was about to begin an apprenticeship in patternmaking. Even the trade, or craft, of patternmaking, meant very little to me, although I had been told that it involved working with wood. Not joinery though, nor

Bob Lishman preparing patterns for despatch and Bob Davison making a pattern for a cast iron drip chute for the Melting Shop Furnaces.

Ted Capstick (machinist) and George Ingram dressing timber on a 24 inch planing and thicknessing machine.

cabinetmaking and not even carpentry, but rather a unique craft that called for more than a little skill. I quelled the rising apprehension by telling myself that this was what an apprenticeship was designed for – to learn and somehow acquire that skill. And, I further consoled myself, hadn't I always loved woodwork?

Joining The Throng

Turning the corner at the Station Hotel (now renamed The Cricketers), I could see the large sheds of the Consett Iron Company's fabrication department at the end of the road. Before long I had reached the Tin Mill Road and had joined a throng of ironworkers hurrying to clock-on. It was at this point that I became aware of the huge complex that Consett Iron Company indeed was. On both sides of the road, black and grey sheds loomed and in the distance, lay my first destination, the general office. From there, I was directed towards what was to be my place of work – the Pattern Shop.

Before me, lay what seemed to me to be miles and miles of twisted railway lines that snaked and branched off into numerous cavernous, corrugated buildings. My first impression was that here was a firm that had given its all to produce as much as possible in the recently fought six-year war and a lack of track maintenance was evidence of this fact. As I picked my way over the rails and passed the entrance to one massive shed, which I later found to be the Melting Shop, I caught a fleeting glimpse of the interior. A swaying train of hot ingot moulds, pulled by a belching, straining locomotive, had barred my way momentarily, giving me the opportunity to look further. Inside this huge cavern, I glimpsed what can only be described as a scene from Hell. White-hot, molten metal was pouring into a large container and illuminating the darkness. Sparks leapt into the air and cascaded on to the rails beneath, while on the gantry above, ghostly figures were silhouetted.

With the way clear, I hurried on and found myself leaving the heat and clamour behind somewhat. Crossing a railway bridge above another railway, I paused to look back. A line of tall chimneys lay alongside the melting shop and overlooked an embankment and the sunken track that ran beneath the bridge. Were these the same chimneys that two years or so before had been the scene of an extraordinary, but ultimately sad piece of flying skill? A Spitfire pilot was reputed to have flown between those very same chimneys the morning before he tragically crashed at the bottom of a field behind the old Vicarage football ground. The railway line beneath the chimneys was the main Consett line, I was to realise, skirting the works on its way to Blackhill and on through the Derwent Valley.

Drop-Legs

My destination, the Pattern Shop, with a cluster of buildings alongside it, was now in sight on the other side of the line, perched on top of the high embankment. With the main body of the works behind me, crossing that bridge brought a sense of relief, for here it was like stepping into the countryside. It was relatively quiet, birds were singing and even tall grass and weeds grew between the heaps of scrap iron that littered the ground. Suddenly a loud thud that seemed to shake the earth beneath my feet, shattered the stillness and silenced the bird song. The noise came from beneath a strange three-legged contraption, which stood a short distance away from the Pattern Shop. I later learned that scrap iron placed beneath the tall legs was broken-up by raising a large steel ball to the apex of the legs, from where it was dropped on to the scrap. A simple idea, but very effective and I was to become accustomed to hearing that thud regularly, over the next few years. The men operating the 'drop-legs', two brothers I believe, took refuge in a dome-shaped, steel shelter, whenever the ball was to be released.

The Raw Apprentice

Before me now was what was to be my future workplace with its big double-door at the front-end of the long, single-storey, brick building. Nervously, I lowered my head and stepped inside by way of a small access door provided in the larger one. I had been told to report to the manager, a Mr Syd Unsworth and I was soon directed to a small, half-glass, office, immediately on my left. The smell of pinewood had been my first impression of the Pattern Shop on entering,

Bill Johnson and Clive Pooley.

Eric Jones sign writing in the Painters' Shop.

and then, the numerous large, bright lights hanging from the rafters, above rows of benches down either side of the shop, had drawn my attention. I would come to realise how necessary good light was in this particular shop, very soon. Mr Unsworth, a genial, stoutly built man, quickly had me feeling more at ease and told me that I would be working with an older apprentice who would show me the ropes. Thus I met Eddie Caygill, a small, quiet lad, a year or so older than myself, who took his new supervisory job seriously, I was pleased to find. The friendliness I then encountered from each man I came into contact with, quickly put me at ease as we commenced a tour of the shop. Here were strangers who went out of their way to greet the new, raw apprentice in their midst and make him feel welcome.

Pattern Shop Machinery

Feeling very self-conscious in my brand-new 'bib and brace' overalls, I took note of the machinery I knew that I would have to operate, in time. There was a large circular saw at the bottom end of the shop and a few yards away, a 24-inch planer and thicknesser. Across from this machine was a large, 15-inch lathe, which stood in line with a smaller 6-inch model. Continuing up that side of the shop, a large coke fire burned and provided heating. Next was a 36-inch diameter sanding-disk, complete with a drum for interior radius sanding. Immediately behind the sanding drum was a guillotine.

In the middle of the shop, a short distance from the sander, a 36-inch diameter bandsaw stood. Immediately opposite was a second fire providing heat. Benches, complete with large, woodworking vices, filled the rest of the space on either side and between them and against the walls, sat the patternmakers' toolboxes, or chests. These plain, black-painted chests were a joy to behold when the lids were lifted. The interiors of each were designed and constructed by the owners, especially to stow the multitude of tools needed in their craft. Tiers of shallow draws held chisels, gouges, twist-bits and other small tools, while planes of all sizes and shape had their special place in the bottom of the chests. The interior of the lids held the handsaws required, both large and small. The owners' initials, painted on the front of each chest, added a final personal touch. Strategically placed on one or two of the window ledges, electrically heated gluepots stood.

Apprentice Brian Thompson working on a six-inch model lathe in 1959.

The Painters' Shop

Our next stop was a small room tacked on to the end of the Pattern Shop. Here I met the painters and their foreman, Bob Millar. Assisted by Eric Jones and Robson Fewster, jobs undertaken by these skilled men were signwriting, French polishing, decorating and probably numerous other 'outside' jobs, unknown to us. I was to enjoy my visits to the painters, as the weeks went on, for here we were supplied with shellac and methylated spirit, which were mixed to make polish for finishing patterns. On my short stays there, I would admire the steady hands of these men as they skilfully painted the letters on signs of every style and size.

The Joiners' Shop

A rail spur ended in the yard outside and on the other side of it, opposite to the Pattern Shop, stood the Joiners' Shop. Here I was introduced to men who were equally friendly and skilled at their job. One man based in this shop was the machine man, Ted Capstick. Ted kept all the machines in good working order and sharpened the saw blades, planer blades and changed them and the sander disks when required. This was, of course, a very responsible job, I came to realise, for blunt blades were dangerous to the user and these machines ran at very high speeds. He was also responsible for the stock of hardware needed for joinery, such as hinges, locks, handles of all types and numerous fixing items.

The Circular Saw

Ted was an expert at operating one of the most dangerous machines in the Pattern Shop too, as he was to demonstrate many times in the coming years. This was of course the large circular saw. Balks of pitchpine had sometimes to be ripped-up and because of their size – probably 12-inches square – and length, great care had to be taken or the saw blade would overheat. When this happened, with the timber ripped partway through and gripping the blade, the blade would heat up, buckle and go out of true, making a fearsome noise as the teeth caught the guides. With a couple of labourers helping him to handle these large balks of timber, Ted would use wedges to keep the ripped timber slightly apart to enable the blade to run relatively free. When the blade did buckle, it had to be kept running without cutting, until it cooled off and ran true again.

Clocking On

One of the joiners I remember well was Bobby Elsdon who was to ride pillion behind me on a long and cold weekend trip to Wembley in 1951, when Newcastle beat Blackpool in the FA Cup Final. Other names which spring to mind in that busy shop were, Stan Capstick (Ted's brother), Fred Wardle, Eric Raine, Wally Lee, Eddie Dodd and Alan Hewitt, who lived near me at Blackfyne. I especially remember Alan, for he and I made a habit of running to work most mornings in order to beat the time-office clock, until I acquired a motor cycle in later days. Three minutes leeway was allowed for clocking on or we lost a quarter of an hour from our pay.

A Master Craftsman

At the end of the Joiners' Shop, was an adjoining room, which made the building into an L-shape. Here worked Eric Raine's father, a man I came to admire immensely. His many years at the craft had made him a master joiner and it was so obvious that he loved his work. Not for him was it necessary to down tools at tea breaks. He would work on, drinking his tea in the process. A kindly old man with a ready smile, Albert had a great interest in natural history, I believe. At the end of the room, a short distance

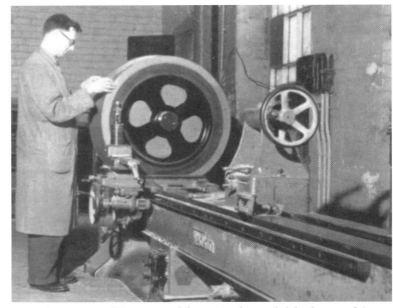

Reg Pierson working on a fifteen-inch model lathe, making a pattern for a cast-iron cable drum for 7$1/2$ ton cranes.

away from Albert's bench, was a corner where the hammer-shafter worked. It was not only hammers of all shapes and sizes, for different departments in the works, that were shafted here, for shovels, picks and all manner of tools needing shafts were brought in to be attended to. Shunting poles were also in great demand.

The Pattern Store

Behind this building was the timber shed, its side open to the air to allow ventilation and access to the stacks of dry and drying timber. Immediately opposite was the Pattern Store; a moulder's Aladdin's cave containing patterns and core boxes for almost anything that needed casting. Bob Lishman, one of the older patternmakers, could expertly find any item needed for the foundry, from the stock of old

George Dickenson (plater), Bill Walton (burner) and Joe Cain (helper), effecting repairs at the Melting Shops.

patterns that filled every shelf from floor to ceiling. When one was needed for dispatch, the ground behind the store was littered with packing cases of all sizes. Bob, I quickly found, was a sort of father figure to me. A quiet man, he always had a joke to tell and had been a decent footballer in his youth. Tennis was now his great love and I could imagine him being an excellent coach to the young players at his Shotley Bridge Club. This, then, was what was known as the Pattern Shop, where not only patterns were made, but also numerous other trades were involved in those other buildings and elsewhere in the works and all under the control of Mr Unsworth.

There was one other brick building a few yards from the Pattern Shop. This was the communal toilet, or lavatory. This was my first encounter of this sort of facility and one that took a while for me to use. Eventually however, there was no other choice and I overcame my embarrassment and took the plunge, so to speak. Strange to say, after a while, it seemed the most natural thing in the world to sit and converse with perhaps three or four others alongside.

Acclimatisation

I was given two days to get used to my new environment and I used the time to ask a multitude of questions, no doubt, for on most of the patternmakers' benches was a part-made pattern. I noted that each man worked from a blueprint, supplied by the drawing office draughtsmen. Not only that, but the drawing had to be transferred full-size, to a perfectly level, suitably sized, purpose-made, drawing board, before any patternmaking could begin.

Dimensions from the blueprint were transferred to the drawing board by using a contraction rule, which meant that the finished pattern was just slightly oversize, to allow for contraction when the resultant casting had cooled, at the company's Crookhall Foundry.

My questions, I found, were occasionally interrupted by Mr Unsworth asking me to take letters, etc to the company's dispatch office, for this was a task to be undertaken by the youngest apprentice. I didn't mind this in the least though, for I was able to explore the works and get acquainted with Miss Moore, the charming, middle-aged lady in charge of the dispatch office and her attractive, young ladies!

Ask For A Job!

After my two days of acclimatisation, naturally, I was keen to make something, or at least attempt to. The practice was to knock at the office door and ask for a job, I was told. Mr Unsworth duly obliged and I returned to my allocated bench, bearing my first blueprint. I studied the plan, side view and end view drawings with absolutely no idea of where to begin. The pattern required was for a half, brass bearing. Obviously, this was a simple pattern to make and a fitting one to help an apprentice to get acquainted with some of the tools and machinery. 'Look for a suitably sized drawing board, plane off the old 'scribed' drawings and make sure it is planed level,' I was told. Many hours later, I was ready to begin drawing with a contraction rule, square, marking gauge, dividers and scriber, all borrowed from Eddie.

To cut a long story short, I proceeded to make the pattern, from teak, as I was told and after being shown how to hold the turning tools managed to produce what I thought was a superb-looking piece of work in the 6-inch lathe. There was just one snag however, for in one small part of the pattern's diameter, I had turned off just a fraction of an inch too much. 'Never mind, just finish polishing it with shellac; Ernie (the chargehand at that time) might pass it,' was the advice. Ernie Purvis didn't pass it however and I learnt a valuable lesson in being accurate. Needless to say, I had to make that brass again, but this time, I made sure that the dimensions were correct.

Timber

After that first experience of working with teak, I became acquainted with a timber that was a joy to work with. This was the wood that most patterns were made of, namely yellow pine. Straight-grained and easy to work, yellow pine was a delight to carve, plane, cut and sand. When given a coat or two of shellac polish, it took on a rich golden colour and because of its stability when properly seasoned, it was an ideal timber for making patterns. After, and because of the war, hardwoods such as teak were in short supply and expensive, and other substitute timbers were tried, such as iroko. This was a difficult wood to work though, due to its unreliable grain.

Mr Unsworth.

Acquiring Tools

As the weeks went by and my apprentice wage of £1 17s 6d (£1.87^1/$_2$) was received, I began to buy one tool each week from Davidson's shop in Consett. There I found that they stocked almost anything in the way of tools that a company apprentice would need. A Sorby chisel would perhaps cost about 3/6d (17^1/$_2$p), while a small, Record or Stanley plane would be about 7/6 (37^1/$_2$p). To give an idea of the range of tools needed for patternmaking, I gave 1/6d (7^1/$_2$p) to buy an eighth of an inch-inside ground gouge, from an old patternmaker. Many tools were passed down to the apprentices in this way and it was not unusual for the tool handles to bear two or three stamped names of retired patternmakers. To illustrate this, I was sitting in a large shoe shop, patiently waiting for my wife, in Blackpool about two or three years ago. The old chap next to me remarked that my accent told him that I was from the North East and he asked me, 'Whereabouts?'

Frank Lowes and Fred Stobbs painting exterior steelwork and Benzole tanks at the Fell Coke Works.

'Consett,' I told him.

'Oh, I knew someone who worked there, at Consett Iron Company, he was a patternmaker,' he said.

Of course, I told him that I had been a patternmaker there myself and asked him what his acquaintance's name was.

'Knifton,' he replied and immediately I said, 'Bill Knifton?' As an apprentice, I had seen 'W. Knifton' stamped on many chisels and gouges and had heard much about this retired patternmaker.

A Christmas Tradition

All company apprentices had to attend night classes and before long I had enrolled at Consett Technical Institute and two nights a week were taken up. The engineering course took in English, drawing, maths and science. Then, Jack Hall, shop steward for the patternmakers, invited me to join the United Patternmakers' Union and I was taken by him to the union headquarters in Newcastle, to be made a member. Life as an apprentice patternmaker was not all work, however, and in the run up to that first Christmas, I learnt that the new apprentice or I should say apprentices – for a fun-loving Clive Pooley had joined me by this time – usually made a collecting box. This was to be taken around the shop and the men invited to put in some money for Christmas. Clive and I were instructed to make it a very strong box, which we certainly did, by using 1" thick wood and by gluing and screwing it together. It then had to be painted black and polished, we were told. In the three weeks or so up to Christmas, that box was taken off us, thrown around the shop from man to man, hidden, found, filled with washers and even had large nails hammered into it. Worse still though, it had even to be retrieved from the roaring coke fires, once or twice, but, we persevered in chasing it, for we knew that there was also quite a lot of money in it too.

A Price To Pay

However, everything has a price, and for our Christmas box, the price was for each of us to stand up and sing a song on Christmas Eve. Not only that but we had to finish off with a duet, we were told. I decided that I would sing 'Clementine' and endeavoured to learn the words in time. There was no getting out of it when Christmas Eve arrived and at about 4 pm, a form was put in place for us in the middle of the shop and one by one we sang to the assembled men. Even now, in retirement, I remember my voice shaking as I sang and a sympathetic Jimmy Seaman's voice urging me on. Then it was time for our duet, a carol, I think, and Clive and I stood together on the form. Just before the end of this duet, the shop erupted as a large sack of sawdust was emptied on to us from the rafters above. It was time to open our box now for we had played our part and had provided the entertainment. To our great delight, apart from a stack of washers and such, we found about £15 each in that battered and burnt box.

The following Christmas saw Clive and I repeating the ordeal, accompanied by a new joiner's apprentice, Neil Walton. This time though, we were determined that we would continually keep our eyes open for signs of movement in the roof space. But, by the time that we were into our final carol, we had dropped our guard and once again, down came the sawdust. It was worth it though, for we went home with something like £10 each that night.

Milton Lishman and Jack Johnson painting a tractor at the garage.

Fun And Games

One man continually provided the humour at work, although there was continuous good-natured banter every Monday morning between the Sunderland and Newcastle United biased men. Tommy Locke provided that humour with his antics and quips. Very seldom did I see Tommy in a serious mood. It was said that he had injured his leg in a fall from a roof, which had left him with a limp. He would make great play of this by occasionally greatly exaggerating the limp, as he carried out his labouring job.

Tommy was a sort of Max Wall and Freddy Starr character rolled into one. His humour was endless. I fondly remember him sweeping the shavings from beneath our feet and moving us around as you would horses, while mucking out a stable. One rather plump old patternmaker often suffered the indignity of Tommy blowing his ample rump up, as with a bicycle pump, as he bent over his open toolbox. To that man's credit, he joined in the laughter each time this happened, although it was hard to take exception to Tommy's brand of humour – humour without malice.

As sixteen year-olds, we apprentices naturally enjoyed a bit of fun and I well remember the day after a certain TV act the night before, which featured a man balancing on a short board, which itself was balanced on and across a six-inch diameter roller. The next day Clive and I had turned ourselves a wooden roller and were risking life and limb on it, between the benches.

At 12 noon, we would rush down our sandwiches and join others on the 'cricket pitch' in the narrow space between the timber shed and the pattern store. Wooden bats, cut out on the bandsaw and balls turned in the lathe were easily replaced when they frequently broke. One man especially was responsible for them breaking, for he bowled and batted without mercy. He was a burly, ex-coalman, from Aberdeen, Jock McKenzie. Jock had been acquired by Consett FC as their new centre forward and was employed as a labourer with us. Another footballer in the department was Tommy Lumley, the former Gateshead inside forward.

The Pattern Shop took part in one or two inter-departmental games. One match in particular, between the Fell labourers' pool and us resulted in a 4-4 result. That game sticks in my mind for two reasons. The first one because of a certain labourer, well past his first flush of youth, who turned out in his long, white 'linings' and managed to get his head in the way of a corner kick. No one was more surprised than him, when the ball rocketed into the net. The second reason for me to remember it was the fact that I was in goal!

My Mentors – The Patternmakers

From my bench, at the bottom of the shop, I had Eddie Caygill on the other side to me. Continuing up the right hand side, as far as I remember at that time, were Clive Pooley from The Grove, Bill Russell from Knitsley, Bob Robson, Tommy Potts from Newcastle, Les Robson (an apprentice) from Delves Lane, Ronnie Crowther, also an apprentice called Billy, Jack Hall from Lobley Hill, Bob Davison from Castleside, Jimmy Seaman, and Arthur Whittaker. On the other side were benches occupied by Bob Lishman, Alan who was an older apprentice, Reg Pierson and Norman Surtees. Two other patternmakers were Ernie Purvis, the chargehand and Tim Walton, who became chargehand when Ernie later left to pursue a business interest, I believe.

Bill Russell and Bob Robson, being the men nearest to me, must have suffered more than most by my lack of patternmaking knowledge, but never once do I remember them not having time to give advice when it was needed. They deserve and have my gratitude, as does every man in that department for their kindness and friendship to a young, 'green' apprentice.

'A Five-Mile Sniper!'

The war had ended barely two years previously and I knew that at least two men from the shop had served in the Army. Jack Johnson, a labourer and Jimmy Seaman. Jack had been a gunner and Jim, having been conscripted for six months only, just before the war began, found himself taken prisoner at Dunkirk and in captivity until the end of the war. I remember hearing a friendly 'exchange' between them one day, when Jack said something derogatory about Jim only being an infantryman. Jim immediately shot back with something like, 'You can talk, you were only a five mile sniper!'

Jack Johnson and I were Newcastle United supporters and never missed a home match. We would make the journey to St James' in later years by motor cycle in all weathers and stand with the other 58-60,000 fans – great days Jack!

More than 50 years later, I still remember little things about those friendly men; Bob Davison's passion for vintage motor cycles, Norman Surtees' love of music, games of snooker with Bob Robson, that holiday with Eddie Caygill in the YMCA at Cullercoats, Tommy Potts and his love of draught Bass, Wally Lee and his Vincent motor cycle, which left my 350cc BSA 'standing' on the A1 – all great memories to have.

Bill Collins and Alan Down making a pattern for a cast iron core barrel for a 14 ton ingot mould.

'The Gaffer'

It wasn't too long before I came to realise that Mr Unsworth was 'Syd' to everyone in the shop. Here was a man who commanded respect and received it, but not by ruling with a rod of iron. His presence seemed to be enough to ensure that the work proceeded at the correct pace and the department remained efficient. Never once did I see him raise his voice or look in danger of losing his temper with anyone. At intervals during the day, Syd would rise from his office chair and walk through the shop on his way to speak to the joiners or the painters. He would acknowledge each man and boy with a friendly smile and greeting as he passed their benches.

Syd must have possessed a tremendous knowledge of patternmaking and foundry practice, for he was able to work out contract hours for each job and give advice when needed. This was a far from easy task when each pattern to be made was usually unique. Perhaps the following, as written by Syd Unsworth, explains a little of what patternmaking is all about:

'Patternmaking – This section, established about 1860, is one of the oldest in the Company and it is the birthplace of most machinery. Until the patternmaker begins his work, the machine is merely a design on paper. He is the most highly skilled worker connected with his industry. He seldom, if ever, makes the same type of thing twice, and knowledge is always being acquired. In addition to working from very complicated mechanical drawings with nothing else to guide him, he has to have a thorough knowledge of other ancillary trades. He is an exalted craftsman – the greatest common denominator as well as the least common multiple of industrial production. That patternmakers can be found in all kinds of administrative posts is due largely to their training in their craft. Patterns are made for all classes of castings in cast steel, cast iron and non-ferrous metals ranging from the smallest bearings to all types of ingot moulds and slag ladles.'

I can vouch for the accuracy of this last sentence, for my first job was that small bearing and one of my later jobs was working day and night with senior men to complete a slag ladle pattern. One of these men I remember clearly – Jim Seamen. Jim was the sort of man an apprentice could go to and ask questions about night school subjects, as well as patternmaking. His knowledge of both theory and practice eventually led to him becoming the Company's apprentice supervisor.

A Man's Wage!

August 1952 saw me complete my five-year apprenticeship and I received my first wage as a patternmaker, a magnificent ten pounds, or thereabouts! Any elation that I now felt was quickly tempered however, for about two weeks later, I was being kitted-out at RAF Padgate, in Lancashire, as a National Service airman and receiving a paltry £1 8s 6d (£1.42$^1/_2$) – much less than my first apprenticeship wage. Thus, two long years were to pass before I could return to the Pattern Shop and patternmaking. Although that five-year apprenticeship had served me well and I had learned skills such as carving, turning, the correct use of woodworking tools and machinery, draughtsmanship and some knowledge of mechanical engineering, I had much to learn yet of the making of complicated patterns suitable for casting purposes. This learning process was an ongoing thing that men spent a lifetime at, for every job was different from the one before.

When a business proposition presented itself in 1956, I left behind a host of friends and a camaraderie that I will always remember, but I took with me skills that would stand me in good stead throughout my life.

A DIARY OF THE CLOSURE

December 1979 – December 1980

by John Eyles, Industrial Chaplain

The Reverend John Eyles with two Catholic students in the Plate Mill around 1977. The students were from Usher College and were at the Works on an industrial placement for a term.

Introduction

This is written to record the experience of the closure of the steelworks at Consett as a result of witnessing the event and the events that led up to it. It may appear to reflect some criticism of the fact of closure, but it is more concerned with the experience of it, granted the decision to close had been made. Throughout the period there was continuous contact with trade union representatives and with managers, although at times the more senior members of both these groups were too busy to make conversation. There was no contact with management at the decision making level where the closure itself and, presumably, methods and timing of closure events were decided. The views expressed are my own. They were formed by contact as industrial chaplain with large numbers of B.S.C. employees at all levels in Consett Works, and by reflection upon the events that occurred.

Closure Announced, 11th December 1979

Background

The immediate background at Consett to the closure announcement was that the Works had moved into slight profit and some departments had settled into a steady run of record-breaking performances. This had come about through closure of the loss-making Hownsgill Plate Mill (not popular, but accepted for the sake of the Works as a whole), through a slow (too slow for management) and painful (to the unions) reduction in general manning, some technical improvement, and what was widely accepted as being a good effort all round. The workforce had been told on a number of occasions that the key to survival was smooth performance and financial profitability. It looked as if these goals were being achieved.

Yet Consett was always a works where the possibility of closure was felt to lie in the background. From the days of the Benson Report (1970) onwards it was recognised that Consett was seen as a small works in an isolated position and one that B.S.C. probably would close at some time as it pursued development of the large works sited near deep water ports. Not that local

Hounsgill Plate Mill restroom – Among those seen are Lawrence McGeary, Bobby Foreman and Dickie Goldsmith.

people agreed with that strategy, some parts of which were arguable anyway. A small works is more flexible and adaptable than a large one, for example, and Consett was not significantly further from the Redcar Ore Terminal than Ravenscraig is from Hunterston. In any case, the possibility of closure was related to development and expansion. By 1979 it was survival that seemed more important and Consett was doing well in that struggle. Another critical point was further investment. In that direction Consett had a newly re-lined blast furnace not yet blown in and a medium sized development in the Billet Mill only completed in the recent past. Things felt likely to be alright for a year or two.

Closure Rumours

Right at the start the pattern seemed to be set for all that followed. Confusion and uncertainty appeared to

The front cover of a campaign newsletter.

predominate, combined at times with rushed action of great swiftness. Following a Board meeting in London on 27th November rumours began to circulate concerning the probability of the closure of Consett Works. B.S.C. said nothing. On Friday, 7th December, the General Manager at Consett Works was moved 'overnight' to a post at Teesside. It was said later by all concerned that this had nothing to do with closure at Consett. Some could accept that; others could not. Guessed reasons for the move were not hard to find, either personal (leaving sinking ship), or corporate (they moved the one man in management who would have fought like hell to keep the Works open). The truth is hard to find. In any case, this move and the rumours together combined to ferment a good deal of uncertainty and speculation.

Closure Announcement

Amid mounting speculation a meeting of employee representatives was called for 3 pm on Tuesday, 11th December, at which the Divisional Director would be speaking. Notice of this meeting was very short. The secretary of the Works Consultative Council was still trying to contact some representatives by phone as late as 12.20 pm on the afternoon of the meeting.

As he opened the meeting, the Divisional Director apologised for the rumours and said it was now time to end them, but unfortunately not happily for Consett. Against a background of reduced demand B.S.C. would be reducing annual output to 15 million tonnes and in order to increase loading and manpower productivity at larger works closures were necessary, including that of Consett Works, which would now have to be negotiated.

The announcement was received with a reaction of shock. Only four questions were asked. These included a query as to how a reversal of the decision might be sought – to which the reply was, there is no way! Lack of demand is the problem. The date of closure was asked, but that had not been decided and the latter part of next year (1980) was all that could be indicated.

Immediate Reaction

The response of the first few days turned Consett into a cauldron of emotions and reactions of every kind. Individuals experienced anger, disbelief and a wide variety of physical symptoms of ill health.

Mr Derek Hume, Shift Manager 'B' letter shift, Steel Plant.

Different unions groups expressed all out resistance to closure seen as a betrayal of efforts of the recent past, or proposed acceptance of Consett and its people as a good workplace for new industry.

A few days later this immediate reaction began to decline. There were few hard facts with which to grapple. More records were broken. Christmas was coming and after that the threatened national strike. It was business as usual for a few more days at any rate.

Time Out – The National Strike, 2nd January – 1st April 1980

The Strike

This might be described as the strike no one wanted, but in the approach to which several groups so acted as to make it inevitable. The expressed reason for the strike was pay – a perceived offer of 2% being taken as an insult. It was said later that the offer was never only 2%, but this perception was allowed to stand for a long time and it may have been allowed, or used, to cloud a deeper issue of control and involvement at divisional rather than national level. Certainly Consett did not want the strike. In a plant under threat of closure it was felt to be an inappropriate strategy. There was anger that this did not appear to have been taken into account nationally, and anger at what was felt to have been ineffective consultation between union leadership and members before calling the strike. Too late, from some people's point of view, it was realised that full authority to call a strike on behalf of I.S.T.C. had been vested in the executive committee of the union, without the need for any kind of ballot. Inexperience or apathy may have contributed to that having happened. There had been no national strike since 1926 and thoughts of how to organise one were not in many member's heads.

So the strike began. Not all unions joined it at the start, and when the craft unions came out there was some debate as to whether they had been laid-off or had joined the strike. That was largely settled by DHSS attitudes to craft workers seeking benefits.

Differences at the start of the strike and different immediate reactions to the threat of closure both contributed to union groups being separated from one another. It was nearly two months after the strike began before all the unions came together to form a joint co-ordinating committee to resist closure. To a large extent the period of the strike was 'time out' from the effort to respond collectively to the intended closure.

For management, too, it was largely a period of time out. Many contingency plans were considered and discarded. Attempts were made to consider various work and loading patterns in an effort to save the Works but no plans appeared to be made about the closure.

Consett March, 14th March 1980

Ten weeks into the strike and one of the first events organised by the joint union co-ordinating committee was the demonstration march around the centre of Consett. It was designed, as much as anything, as a community event for a wide cross-section of people to join in. The town community was encouraged to express concern and involvement in taking hold of its own destiny and in claiming the steelworks as an ongoing part of its heritage. Some $2^1/2$ to 3 thousand people joined in the march and the route was lined with many more.

Given the length of the strike and the presence of national union leaders, the march was amazingly good humoured, as was the rally afterwards in two local cinemas. Strike issues were almost universally ignored and response to the intended closure was the only item on the agenda. And now the polemic began to emerge. Possible political intrigue with private industry on the part of the government, and plain bad faith towards Consett Works on the part of B.S.C. were among the accusations raised.

At most only one or two members of Consett management would have heard the speeches. But then they were not thought to be the real adversary. The real adversary was felt to be rather more remote and inaccessible.

And the real adversary was thought to be putting pressure on its local agents not to get involved in the closure debate, only to administer it in due course. Some later conversations tended to confirm this allegation.

It is interesting to note how quickly adversary language and accusations of bad faith come to the fore in situations of this kind.

The town gets behind the campaign.

Being suddenly faced with impending closure, it is not surprising that this becomes part of trade union comment, especially where apparent reversals of previous policy seem to be involved. But management comment and feelings were sometimes in the same vein as well. Would it be feasible to approach a possible closure situation in any different way?

Waiting And Rumours

At the beginning of April work resumed and got back to normal surprisingly quickly. By the end of the month records once again being broken. On or about 9th April a meeting with trade union representatives was called by the Divisional Director. Having adopted a stance of non-co-operation with management over closure, I.S.T.C. delegates did not attend. The intention

Jim Lawson, Raw materials Controller, 'A' letter shift, Steel Plant.

was expressed of publishing a booklet or brochure setting out the detailed case for closure of the Works. Attempts to discuss the likely questions such a brochure should try to answer met with little response. It was said the brochure would be published about a month later. In fact over two months elapsed before the brochure appeared.

In that time a great deal of speculation and unease arose. 'When will they tell us the date?' was the widespread cry. Neither work nor private life could be planned in the face of such total uncertainty.

Many people, perhaps a very large majority, wanted the Works to remain open, but they wanted an open future not a day to day existence. Closure was preferable to that. Some even wondered if delay and uncertainty were being used deliberately to undermine morale.

In the absence of precise intentions on the part of B.S.C. there was also an absence of a clear policy on the part of the unions. There was generally union opposition to closure on the grounds that the Works were profitable and that closure would cause untold social harm. A more detailed elaboration of how a case might be argued was not presented. People began to wonder how far they could support a general blanket opposition to closure. Yet initiative appeared to lie with B.S.C. Until they published the grounds on which closure had been decided, how could arguments be refuted or alternatives be proposed.

During that time also, on 28th April, a phoney and seemingly unreal meeting of the Works' Consultative Council was held. The basic facts centred on reduced demand were again presented as laying behind the closure decision. Then most of the meeting was taken up with discussing details of the added value bonus scheme that was part of the recent national agreement. Important though that was, even for its possible impact on redundancy pay, to discuss at length a scheme for future patterns of payment against the expectation of imminent closure felt so unreal that one member described it as industrial schizophrenia. Again, I.S.T.C. were not present, which only added to the air of unreality.

The Case For Consett Closure

The Brochure

About two months after first being mentioned, the brochure setting out the case for closure of Consett Works was presented at a meeting of representative managers and employees called by the Divisional Director on 12th June 1980. It contained no real surprises, reduced demand being still presented as the significant factor. It was said that demand was still reducing, a fact born out in the course of time. Billet and billet derived products were particularly hard hit by the decline in the motor industry and in engineering. Closing Consett Works would save B.S.C. an estimated £40.5 million annually. Its order load could be re-allocated elsewhere in B.S.C. and so the Corporation announced its intention to cease operations at its Consett Works from 30th September 1980.

There was virtually no discussion, the union representatives through their chairman asking for an adjournment for three or four weeks in order to make a considered response in similar brochure form.

The next day I received a copy of the brochure and was surprised at the fairly elaborate procedures to account for all copies and to consider them confidential. I would have thought that a widespread distribution would have been wanted with direct access to copies for the majority of people affected, so that they might appreciate the arguments presented.

Response

The immediate response on shop floor and in offices was of some relief at knowing the date and in understanding, as the brochure stated, that two blast furnace production was intended up to the time of closure. This was also a time for criticism, some of it quite specific, of both management and unions for allowing the situation to develop in the way it had over the years so that closure had to be considered at all. Some of this might have been scape-goating. Through all this, the feeling seemed to be growing that the closure would happen now, as planned, and little or nothing could stop it.

Nevertheless a mass meeting of employees on the local football ground on

Hounsgill restroom after the closure.

20th June unanimously supported the joint union co-ordinating committee in seeking to obtain a profitable, long term future for the Consett Works. Some 300 people were present. At this meeting the beginnings of a union alternative strategy were seen starting to emerge. This turned on proposing a move up market in terms of product to an area said to be served by imports and capable of yielding £7.5 million profit in Consett Works in a full year.

Alternatives

No Case For Closure

The Trade Union Alternative Strategy for Consett Works was published as a brochure early in July. It was a disappointing document, not seeming to reach heights or depths of analysis somehow promised in public speeches. Its arguments focused around moving up market for billet production and being a back up for Teesside, especially at times of relining the Redcar blast furnace. Although the arguments were not very fully developed they appeared to deserve a hearing and an answer. This, at least, has been born out by later events in that rapidly escalating costs of electricity make the electric arc route very unattractive for products which could be made in any other way.

It was intended to present the brochure and its arguments to the Division and to the Board of B.S.C., but no dates were clearly set for doing that. A meeting with divisional management, the adjourned meeting of 12th June, was held on 7th July, but only a verbal response was offered in reply to the June brochure. It was said that the Alternative Strategy would first be presented to and within T.U.C.S.I.C. Just what was the general strategy here is not easy to determine, but it does appear to have contributed to the delays in effective communication which from here on in influenced everything that took place. T.U.C.S.I.C. held a meeting in Consett on 10th July and that seems to have been the effective date of publishing the Alternative Strategy.

London March, 9th July 1980

In the meantime a London march had been organised to carry Consett claims for re-consideration of closure policies, to parliament. It was a lively but orderly affair with band playing, leaflets flying, and almost a carnival atmosphere, despite its serious intent. The march was welcomed at

Bill Stephenson, Casting Bay Controller, 'C' letter shift, Steel Plant, Consett.

Westminster by nearly all the opposition front bench and all the northern group of Labour MPs. This warmth may have been just as political in its way as was the absence of any member of other parties and the difficulty in getting other than Labour MPs to come to the lobby in response to personal requests sent into the House.

This was felt to be an essential exercise. It gained wide publicity for Consett outside the local area. But did it achieve anything else? And how much real support did it have? It is hard to judge its total

'B' shift letter, Steel Plant L.D. Vessel crew and others including: Jack Northey, Bobby Robinson, 'Mal' Reed, Jimmy Fell, Tommy Williamson (casting bay), Ronnie Teasdale and Dave Broadley (fume hood attendants).

impact, and support from the community was more of interest than of ready participation. It is quite hard to fill a train with 600 people.

More Waiting; More Uncertainty

Meetings

Now began a very trying time for all employed at Consett Works. There always appeared to be a meeting in the offing which would be decisive, meaning that the Alternative Strategy would be accepted or refuted at the highest level by B.S.C. management. Meetings on 23rd July at Ladgate Lane, Teesside, with huge police surveillance, and on 12th August in London, both came and went without that decisive point being felt to have been reached. The Chairman and Chief Executive kept a low profile and did not appear, as I understand it, at either meeting.

As time went by reaction against the continuing union stance of opposition to closure began to grow. People came to feel that proper opposition to closure had been expressed, but had not been successful in changing policy, and so negotiating closure was the appropriate activity now. The union committee itself, organised since May as a mini steel committee (Reflecting T.U.C.S.I.C. structure) and very busy since that time, began to feel in a state of limbo.

There was no more initiative they could take, yet they did not feel they had reached the point where it was appropriate to change course. It was a matter of waiting. In spite of growing pressure to change, they succeeded in retaining support for continuing resistance to closure up until a further meeting in London on 29th August. While the waiting was going on other events were taking place.

Second Consett March, 25th July 1980

This was an anti-climax after the earlier Consett march and the London march. Only about 1500 people took part and too many union and political speeches were made on the rugby ground at a rally at the end of the march. People simply melted away, symbolising the reduced support for the campaign generally.

Summer Shutdown, 26th July – 10th August

Blast furnaces were banked for the shutdown in the usual way, but the usual programme of repairs and maintenance across the Works was not carried out. When the holidays were over, only one furnace was brought back on. So much for the intended two furnace production up until closure hoped for in the June brochure.

Redundancy Counselling

This began in earnest in July, before the summer shutdown and continued at a frantic pace all through August. It took place despite union opposition which looked on the acceptance of counselling as tacit acceptance of closure. A 'belt and braces' approach which most people wanted did not seem to be a philosophy which union representatives could support.

Neville Hutchinson, Shift Manager, 'C' letter shift, Steel Plant, Consett.

Pressure of time and of numbers and the general atmosphere of the Works was not conductive to counselling at any depth. Most people sought and gained information about the nature of payments which might be made, and a general indication of re-training possibilities. There were criticisms later of the inadequacy of counselling, but it is hard to see how a more thorough-going exercise could have been carried out given all the constraints at the time. There emerged a need for post-redundancy counselling after the Works.

An attempt was made to make Newport & Gwent Industrial Mission's book, 'Redundant? A Personal Survival Kit', widely available. Several hundred copies were ordered by Consett Works, but it was decided to put a small charge on the books to give them value to the recipient beyond being just 'another piece of paper'. In the event B.S.C. counsellors became unwilling to handle this. In the face of union opposition to the service as such they were unwilling to appear to be selling anything. Subsequently a good many copies were released into the community via the Northumbrian Industrial Mission.

Closure, 29th August – 13th September

London Meeting, 29th August

The long awaited meeting between T.U.C.S.I.C. and B.S.C. including the Chairman of B.S.C. took place on the evening of Friday, 29th August. The meeting opened in the knowledge that Mr MacGregor had been reported as saying he had no intention of discussing Consett any further. Nevertheless, a Consett delegation was present and T.U.C.S.I.C. attempted to present a plan for more voluntary redundancies in return for keeping open the Consett Works. It was said in reply there was no possibility of this and in fact the closure must be brought forward. Steel making would end 'next weekend'. At least that is what was reported. Only later was it made clear that this meant 12th and 13 September.

The First Week Of Closure Preparation, 1st – 5th September

It took a couple of days for all concerned in decision-making, action and negotiation to adjust to the very short time scale of 9/10 working days instead of the full month thought to remain. In that time it emerged that the last shift of iron making, steel making and rolling would be on Friday, 12th September; the last coke oven would be pushed on 13th September; the last shift worked to 21 shift pattern would be that ending at 6 am on Sunday, 14th September.

During this week it became clear that some 40-45 fourth year apprentices would be signed off as their apprenticeships expired on 5th September. At first it was expected they would just leave empty-handed, having no entitlement to any payments, but local negotiations agreed ex-gratia payments of £900 each.

On Wednesday, 3rd September, a mass meeting was held at the Works at which the mini steel committee reported the London meeting of 29th August and other meetings with local management. It was said that the mass meeting was held only in the face of great opposition from local management, yet it was a dignified, orderly meeting which was very moving. Two resolutions were passed, one 'bitterly resenting wrongful closure of the Works, but facing reality, seeks to negotiate the best possible terms of closure', the other placed negotiations, 'in the hands of T.U.C.S.I.C. in liaison with the local mini steel committee'. Both were passed overwhelmingly, votes being of the order of 2000 to 20 in each case.

By now, undoubtedly, there were some people who could not wait to get out and receive the money they felt sure would be coming their way. Others voted with a sense of relief that nine months of rumour, uncertainty and frequent changes in plans could now be brought to an end. The anxiety had seemed like a Chinese water torture and they longed for it to end. Yet many realised that in raising their hands to accept negotiations, although they had no power to do otherwise, they were voting to end the only way of life they knew. It was very hard. Perhaps that is why it was such a dignified, human event.

Also during this week, and for several weeks to come, there began to be reported news of a possible private consortium interested in taking over the Works. Not many local people gave the possibility much credence. Neither management nor unions had any clear knowledge of the group. But they did achieve quite a lot of publicity and enough response from B.S.C. in London for the blast furnaces to be banked for two weeks beyond 12th September before finally being quenched. To some people it seemed just one more uncertainty with which to be tormented.

Mr Robert (Bob) Atkinson, Steel Plant Manager for many years.

The Closure Agreement, 8th – 9th September

The second week opened with closure negotiations on the Monday between some 6 members of B.S.C. management, including the Industrial Relations Director from London and some 26 union representatives from T.U.C.S.I.C. and the local mini-steel committee. Clearly there was pressure of time, but also there was strong pressure on the part of management to conclude agreement within the one meeting. This was achieved late in the evening, but granted the desperate aims of the parties to the negotiations it is not, perhaps, surprising that the agreement was later found to be far from satisfactory. Neither local management nor the local workforce obtained from the agreement what they might have hoped.

News of the agreement began to circulate on the Tuesday, the severance payments being understood as; 25 weeks pay on leaving, plus 25 weeks on the anniversary of the closure; 10 weeks holiday pay; up to 12 weeks pay in lieu of notice. In addition, of course, there would be the appropriate redundancy pay which would be boosted to 50% above the statutory scheme by the European Coal and Steel Community. Not everyone was satisfied, especially with the delayed payment of half the severance pay. Most people were relieved that a deal had been made and one more uncertainty was out of the way. No one noticed that no mention had been made of Hownsgill Plate Mill employees. That mill had closed a year earlier on far less favourable terms and with the idea then mooted that if the main works should close in the reasonably near future some review of those terms might be in order. Apparently neither unions nor management raised this issue in negotiation.

Anger And Confusion Abound, 10th – 11th September

The remainder of the week became one appalling turmoil of uncertainty and anxiety. The nearer it came to the time of closure, the less a person felt sure precisely what was his or her position and what was expected of them. By the Thursday evening at 5 o'clock no one had received notice terminating their employment, yet everyone knew work was ending the next day and many people had seen notices on departmental managers' desks, as I had done. But they could not be delivered.

Ferguson (Fergie) Tait, First Hand Vessel man, 'A' letter shift, Steel Plant, Consett.

I was told later by the General Manager that I was greatly mistaken in thinking that notices were to hand but not allowed to be issued. They just were not ready until the Thursday evening and that is why they were not issued sooner. My notes of conversations and clear recollection reveal otherwise. However, the point now is not the precise situation in this regard, but the way it tends to illustrate the impossible pressures of attempting to implement closure in two weeks. Normal patterns of communication broke down. For lack of clear information some procedures may have been carried out in ways other than those intended. Very few people knew what was going on. The personal uncertainty was agonising.

The focus of all this was a

Back row, left to right: Tommy Williamson, Derek Lee, Phil Stokoe (casting bay), John McKean (crane driver). Front row: W. Thompson (casting bay), Malcolm Agnew (crane driver), Derek Hutchinson (remembered as 'Bald Eagle' – vessel crew & technical support).

requirement for some people to work on to accomplish various run-down procedures and administer the clearance of the site, taken together with the outworking of the closure agreement.

The agreement was taken to mean that those staying would work their notice (receiving wages less taxes, etc) while those leaving would receive an ex-gratia payment in lieu of notice (wages in one sum with no deductions). Further, anyone working after December 1980 would receive less severance pay at the rate of $1/2$ week for every week worked.

This was universally interpreted to be a grievous loss to anyone who stayed. Despite the fact that gross receipts over time might be greater than the severance pay alone, the fact that the cash-in-hand on leaving to face an uncertain future would at that moment be less, was taken to be wholly unacceptable, especially as staying on would be an open-ended arrangement with no idea of a date of leaving.

Virtually no-one wished to stay. Yet volunteers were needed and short of receiving volunteers, departmental managers were required to determine lists of people to stay in appropriate categories. Until lists were agreed, no one could be told who was going and who was staying. Some managers who had begun working on such lists a little early, before the full impact of what was understood from the agreement became known, felt they had been led into betraying the best interests of their good workers whom they had been inclined to list or encourage to volunteer, expecting extra work to be some kind of bonus. There appeared to be a complete impasse.

It was resolved by some hard local bargaining. It became agreed that a person would only receive a tax free sum in lieu of notice. A phrase in the agreement to the effect that volunteers only required after December 1980 was taken to be of great significance by the unions who pressed that point and referred it to their full-time officials for ratification. Thus lists were prepared of greater or less willing volunteers; notices were issued; most people were able to leave. They left with a sense of relief mixed with pain. In losing their

An aerial view of the Works, circa 1961.

employment people suffered many losses, not all of which were appreciated until later. Many left with a sense of distress at the abrupt and unceremonious ending of near on a lifetime of work with one organisation.

Closure, 12th – 13th September

These were strange days combining an atmosphere a bit like Christmas Eve together with a great enormous sadness. Photographers and samplers abounded. Official photographers and press photographers were busy recording the last 'everything'. Work people were busy photographing each other in groups and everyone was after a last sample. The last tap of the blast furnace was followed by the last cast of steel. The last ingot was rolled to billets and all production ceased. On the Friday evening a piper played a lament all around the Works. On the Saturday the last coke oven was pushed. The blast furnaces remained banked for two weeks until it was clear the private consortium could not take on the Works. The power station ran on until 24th October, but to all intents and purposes the Works closed this weekend and about 3000 people went out of the gates for the last time.

After Closure

The account of how people began to sort out their affairs and plan towards the future is another story. A few, mainly well qualified, found alternative work and moved to it. A few hundred entered re-training courses of many kinds. Some (over 55s) could treat it as early retirement. The majority just had to wait and see and think and ask about anything and everything that might be possible.

On Sunday, 5th October, an ecumenical service was held in Consett Parish Church organised by all the Christian ministries active in the centre of the town. Readings and hymns provided expression of anger, faith and thanksgiving in reflecting on 'Consett Steel 1840-1980'. The sermon encouraged confidence and endeavour towards the future. Many people attended the service which was the only public event in the community to acknowledge the closure.

The first demolition, of a cooling tower, took place on 3rd December, by which time B.S.C. (Industry) Ltd had converted a small set of buildings into seven workshops for private businesses. The site has started to change. On the anniversary of the closure announcement (11th December 1980), the Chairman of B.S.C. met the steel unions in London and spoke of the need for further drastic re-organisation. When details became known the next day they included the closure of Normanby Park in Scunthorpe. The general feeling around Consett was that of relief that Consett had lost the battle with Normanby Park a year ago. If there has to be a closure it is good to get it over. The sooner one is out, the sooner the future can be faced. It is harder for those who come later.

A view of the Works looking south.

Once the Works closed landmarks that once dominated Consett's skyline disappeared. Here we see the demolition of the cooling tower.

The demolition charge has just been detonated and the coal bunker begins to crumble.

The huge storage tank at the Coke Works collapses and slowly gathers momentum towards the ground.

The coal bunker crumples in a cloud of dust.

Before and after the demise of the world famous Consett Works. The 650 acre site of former industrial activity was returned to a more natural glory and landscape beauty.

REMEMBER THE WORKERS

Men and boys who worked at Delves Brickworks and Coke Ovens in 1905.

Bill Wigham, Ernie Telford and Bob Robinson examining the practised performance of the heat of steel just tapped.

Twins Kathryn (left) and Marilyn Smith celebrating their twenty-first birthday on 27th April 1968. Both girls worked in the Data Processing Department, Kathryn as a filing clerk and Marilyn as a punch-card operator. Their dad David Smith worked in the Billet Mill.

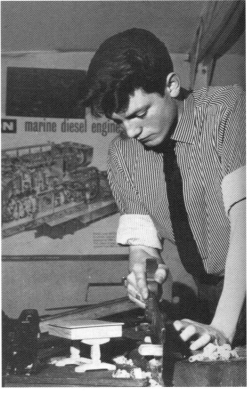

Sixteen-year-old Geoffrey Baird beginning his training as a fitter and turner in 1964.

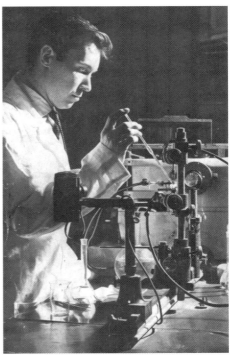

Hard at work at the weighbridge in 1963: George Argue, Tommy Jacques and Arthur Varty.

Spectographer W. Burton at work in the Technical Department in 1966.

Workers relaxing in the Hownsgill Canteen in 1966.

*A Works junior football team, 1957-58. Back row: M. Hutton (Pattern Shops),
A. Bellamy (New Mill), K. Lowes (Engine Sheds), R. Gleghorn (Millwrights),
R. Walton (Engine Sheds), F. Porteous (Plate Mill) and P. Richardson (Cost
Office). Front row: A. Bollands (Plate Mill), J. Dukes (Fitting Shop),
W. Spedding (Blacksmiths' Shop) and B. Smithson (Fell Coke Works).*

*A. Laws (blacksmith) and Barry Cook (striker) bending a hook for a mobile
crane in the 1950s.*

Alan Graham at work in the Drawing Office in 1958

The Drawing Office in the 1950s.

Tracers in the Drawing Office in 1967. Left to right: M. Caswell, G. Brown, J. McDonagh and M. Simpson.

Family and friends having a good night out.

Staff in the Technical Department in 1960.

Left to right: G. Raine (metallurgical technician), G. Carhill (apprentice fitter and turner), A. Bell (apprentice electrician) and T. Douglas (apprentice fitter and turner). All the lads spent time in Germany in 1966 on an apprentice exchange scheme.

W. Jackson and John Dettmer, who worked in the Planning Office, using the Lamsen Tubes and the loud hailer system.

Fifteen-year-olds Robert Johnson (left) and Stuart Bramley – scrapers in the Slabbing, Blooming and Billett Mill in 1960.

Clark Dick at work in the Plate Mill in 1958.

Man and boy – Thomas Arthur Whittaker spent over half a century in the Pattern Shop. He started work at 13 years of age and served his time as a patternmaker (below, front row, second right). In January 1958 he was still at work in the same place 55 years later (right).

The Pattern Shop in the early 1900s. Back row, left to right: G. Hogg, T. Cuthbertson, J. Almond, T. Nixon, W. Knifton, G. Brown, J. Bates and R. Saxty. Second row: T. Campbell, T. Gentiles, F. Watts and J. Stevenson. Third row: J. Watts, R. Lowrie, R. Douglas, J. Kirkup (foreman), J. Gardener and G. Hammond. Front row: W. Parker, P. Watson, W. Suddes, A. Whittaker and G. Willey.

Ladies in the Pay Department in 1959.

*Four Plate Mills workers in 1957. Left to right: R.G. Smith (heater),
M. Loughran (charger driver), W.B. Pattinson (mills clerk) and R. Askew
(shearsman). At the time the photograph was taken the men had put in a total
of 192 years service with Consett Iron Company*

*Rebuilding work at No 12 Soaking Pit in the summer of 1963. Left to right:
G. Turnbull (bricklayers' chargeman), J. Johnson (bricklayer), S. Nattress
(labourer) and J. O'Neil (labourer).*

In the Dispatch Office in 1959 are, standing left to right: Nancy Clark, Dorothy Robson, Valerie Gray, Jeanette Burdon and June Gleghorn. In the centre is Norma Thompson and at the back is Jack Latham, in charge of the department.

Men enjoying a meal in Templetown Canteen in 1966.

Joe Thompson splicing a wire rope in the late 1950s.

Right: Norman Surtees making a pattern for a slag pot for the Foundry.

Tommy Moore watching the last heat tapped from the Consett Steel Plant, 12th September 1980.

Also Available From
The People's History

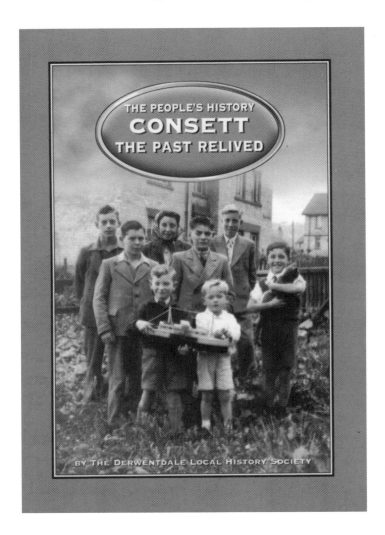

The People's History

To receive a catalogue of the latest titles send a large SAE to:

The People's History Ltd
Suite 1, Byron House
Seaham Grange Business Park
Seaham, County Durham SR7 0PY